Hooked

Hooked

A step-by-step guide to
the fashionable world of crochet

CLAIRE MONTGOMERIE

This edition published by Parragon Books Ltd in 2016

MAKER CRAFTS is an imprint of Parragon Books Ltd

Parragon Books Ltd
Chartist House
15–17 Trim Street
Bath BA1 1HA, UK
www.parragon.com

ISBN 978-1-4748-0418-9

Printed in China

Written by Claire Montgomerie
Projects designed and made by Claire Montgomerie
Edited by Rhian Drinkwater
Technical editing by Rachel Vowles
Pattern charts by Irina Palczynski
Designed and produced by Sue Pressley and
    Paul Turner, Stonecastle Graphics Ltd
Photography by The Photography Firm on location
    at The Tack Barn, Upper Lodge, Sussex, UK

NOTES FOR THE READER
This book uses metric measurements.

Additional photography
Stonecastle Graphics Ltd: *p44 row 2 left; p45; p63; p82; p123.* iStock.com: *p8 row 1 left, row 4 left, row 4 centre; p11 row 1 centre, row 1 right, row 2 left, row 2 centre, row 2 right, row 3 left; p13 row 1 left, row 1 right, row 2 left, row 3 centre, row 3 right, row 4 left, row 4 right; p14 below right; p15 below right; p17 row 4 left; p29 top right; p31.* Shutterstock.com: *p8 row 3 left; p11 row 4 right; p13 row 3 left; p17 row 2 left, row 2 right, row 3 centre, row 3 right; p30.*

CONTENTS

INTRODUCTION

You might have got the impression that crochet is complicated and fiddly, but as you progress through this book – creating beautiful projects to wear and for your home – you will soon discover that crochet is not at all tricky to master.

I have always believed that anyone can learn to crochet, so long as you follow one simple rule: don't try to run before you can chain! When my mother taught me to crochet, she followed her grandmother's lead and helped me to hook metre upon metre of chain before I was shown any further stitches and it was a fantastic foundation for learning the more difficult techniques. Crochet has a wonderfully relaxing and rhythmical flow once you have mastered a comfortable hold and it is only once this flow is achieved that the following stitches become a breeze. Therefore, my number one tip for learning to crochet is to not jump ahead! Make a point of working methodically through the techniques, practising each one thoroughly and then applying them to simple projects – soon the stitches will become familiar and the process will become second nature. All the projects in this book are very simple to create, but are designed to be worked in order, with the projects in the first chapter containing the ideal first projects to tackle, while new techniques and skills are introduced the further you progress.

Each project has been designed to be simple, fun to make and extremely desirable, so that hopefully even more advanced crocheters will enjoy making them too. Thanks to its kitsch past, crochet is sometimes thought of as the slightly less cool sister craft to knitting, but nowadays the tide is beginning to turn, so much so that I am now teaching far more people to crochet than to knit. The granny square is the most requested technique to learn by my beginners, which is not surprising, as it is so easy to work. It uses only the basic treble and chain stitches, the motifs are very portable for on-the-go hooking and the pattern is so adaptable. Perfect for homeware and fashion alike, the notorious granny square is evolving from its past, when it was often a clichéd retro Afghan pattern made in garish clashing colours. There are so many beautifully coloured variations on the internet, which you can browse for inspiration once you have mastered the motif, but for this book I chose a palette that is the antithesis of the multicoloured throws of the past. Soothing neutrals with a pop of colour to highlight the pretty cross in the middle of each motif create a classy blanket perfect for any newborn, or made larger, fabulous in a modern interior.

This understated, classic and fresh theme runs throughout the book to create a covetable collection of modern patterns. One of my personal favourites is the pattern for the Gadget Cosies, which epitomises how good even the most simple crochet fabrics can look. The chunky yarn shows off the most basic of crochet stitches flawlessly to create a satisfyingly crisp fabric, perfect for protecting your delicate electronics, while the striking dash of colour is so easy to create with a simple stripe. Projects like the Chunky Basket Trio, Tiny Coin Purse and Fingerless Gloves demonstrate how easy it is to make seamless, three dimensional fabrics in crochet, which is great news for those of you who do not wish to sew!

Crochet is quick to work, practical, relaxing and easy to adapt. It is also eminently portable, meaning that small projects and motifs are ideal for carrying in your bag for those frequent 'lost' moments waiting in queues or travelling on public transport. Add to this the array of gorgeous, modern patterns available today and I am sure that you will become addicted to this fabulous pastime in no time at all.

Claire Montgomerie

CROCHET BASICS

Discover everything you will need
to begin crocheting with confidence.
From the essential materials and
notions to the techniques and
stitches used in the patterns,
everything is outlined here for easy
reference. You'll also find clear
step-by-step images and handy
tips and tricks to make
learning to crochet a breeze.

TOOLS, NOTIONS & EQUIPMENT

When beginning to crochet, the only essentials are a hook and a ball of yarn. However, there are many tools and notions which can make your crochet life a lot easier. Here is a list of the recommended kit.

CROCHET HOOKS

Crochet hooks come in many materials, shapes and sizes. Choosing which ones to use can be tricky, so we have a simple guide to the different types on page 16. As you become more experienced, you will discover the type of hooks you like to use best.

SCISSORS

Scissors are a must-have when crocheting, to cut yarn when a project is finished and snip yarn ends. Small, sharp embroidery or sewing scissors are best for a quick, clean cut and will fit easily in your crochet bag. It may also be useful to have a pair of good quality, heavy fabric scissors for the occasions when you pair your projects with sewing, for example to cut a lining for a bag.

STITCH MARKERS

When working in the round using double crochet, stitch markers are essential for marking the beginning of a round. They can also be used for marking a specific row or stitch that you will need to refer to later, or to mark the right side of your work. The markers generally come in two versions, as a split ring or a lockable marker.

Split rings are handy for the occasions when you need to move a marker frequently, while lockable ones are great when you need to be sure the marker will not fall out. There is a myriad of fancy markers on the market these days, made in plastic or metal or embellished with beads and fancy decorations.

TAPE MEASURE

Always keep a tape measure close by for checking the tension of your crochet and measuring your work.

NEEDLES

A blunt tapestry or yarn needle is essential for sewing up your crochet neatly. The blunt end ensures that the needle passes through the stitches to create a neat and professional finish without splitting the yarn. These needles come in differing sizes, with varying sized eyes for diverse weights of yarn. There are even some needles available with a 'lip' at the pointy end, which makes it easier to insert behind a stitch.

Sewing needles are also handy for attaching buttons, clasps, beads and other embellishments, as well as for sewing in linings.

PINS

Marking pins are useful for holding two pieces of crochet together while sewing them up, or for pinning the crochet out to shape when blocking. Make sure the pins have a large head so that they do not slip out between the stitches.

POM-POM MAKER

Plastic pom-pom makers offer a fast and easy way to create traditional pom-poms and can save huge amounts of time if you are making multiple pom-poms. They are available in various sizes for pom-poms of different diameters.

CHOOSING YARNS

When new to crochet, take care when selecting the yarn you want to work with. Its construction, as well as the fibre it is made of, can make a lot of difference to how easy it is to crochet.

FIBRES AND CONSTRUCTION

Traditionally, the yarn used for crochet would be a very fine crochet cotton thread. This would usually be mercerised (treated to add strength and lustre) and tightly spun, which makes a thread very strong and unyielding. This is still a great choice for crochet but there are so many different types of yarn and fibre on the market now that you needn't stick to the traditional crochet cotton. In fact, many other yarns can be much easier on your hands than the unforgiving crochet thread. Elastic, warm and comfortable wool and wool mix yarns are just as good as cotton to crochet with.

Wool and cotton are beautiful natural fibres, which are lovely to handle and also have other benefits. Wool regulates your temperature – it has fabulous insulating properties and while keeping you warm in the cold will also help keep you cool in the heat! Wool is anti-bacterial as bacteria tend to prefer smooth surfaces, and it also draws away moisture from the body. All of these properties make it perfect for garments.

Cotton is usually spun with a smooth finish and it is durable, making it perfect for crochet. It is great for summer weight garments as it is cool and breathable and it also takes dye well, so cotton yarns are available in an array of bright, strong shades.

TIP
When using your yarn, it is a good idea to try to pull the yarn from the centre of the ball, rather than from the outside of it, as this will create a steady ball that will not roll around as you crochet.

Man-made yarns were developed to imitate natural fibres, while also compensating for their weaknesses. Therefore they are generally strong, cheap, lightweight, colourfast and moth resistant. However, they often don't feel as soft and tactile as natural fibres. A mix of both man-made and natural can be the best compromise, taking the best from both worlds and ensuring that a yarn can be both beautiful and incredibly durable.

CHOOSE WISELY

If you're new to crochet, take care when selecting the yarn you want for your project. Its construction and the fibre it is made of will influence how easy it will be to work with.

A strand of yarn is made up of different plies – single threads that are spun together to make a stronger, thicker yarn. If these are not spun tightly together, your hook can easily slip inside the plies instead of through the stitch, creating snags and a slow hooking process. To test whether a yarn – whether a cotton or another fibre – is 'splitty', gently twist the yarn in the opposite direction to the way it is spun. If the plies quickly and easily fall apart from each other, the yarn may cause a problem with snagging as you go.

A single ply or roving yarn is often the best to choose when crocheting as it has no plies to catch the hook. A relatively new type of yarn is a cotton jersey stretch that is made from recycled offcuts from the fashion industry. It is strong, bulky and quick to work up, and is perfect for crochet.

The best yarns should be smooth and have no fancy nupps, loops or slubs, so that it is easy to draw through the stitches with your hook and easy to get a good

thickness of yarn is called the weight. The classification of the exact thicknesses will vary from country to country and between brands.

If all this information is a lot to take in, don't worry, most yarns have a yarn band, wrap or tag that will give you all the details you need.

The band will tell you what fibre or mix of fibres the yarn is made from, the weight and the approximate length of the yarn. There may be symbols or written instructions on washing and drying guidelines, and the shade and dye-lot number on the ball band. It is important that all of the yarn for a project comes from the same dye lot. Slight differences in colour may not be immediately apparent in a certain light, but could be horribly obvious in a finished piece.

You should also see a suggested tension and hook size. Often a hook is not shown, just the knitting needle size, but don't despair – you can still use the yarn. Most knitting yarns are suitable for crochet as well, simply try the same size hook as the needle suggested.

stitch definition. Mohair yarns and others that are overly hairy should also be avoided when learning to crochet because the stitches will be hard to make and to see. Also any mistakes made are particularly hard to pull out, as the hairs adhere to one another and knot up.

Chunky yarns and hooks are also good to use when crocheting, but do not fall into the trap of thinking that your first project will be easier and quicker if it is worked in bulky yarn. The movements needed to wield a larger hook are very exaggerated and can wear out your hands more easily. It is far better to practice the basics on a medium weight yarn like a double knit (DK) or Aran/worsted weight yarn, where the stitches will be smaller and the hand movements easier to complete. The

TIP

Sometimes you may buy your yarn in a skein, rather than a ball. If so, make sure that you wind the skein into a ball before using it, otherwise it will get knotted and tangled.

The best way to do this is to get someone to hold the loop of yarn while you wind it into a ball. If you don't have a willing helper handy, then simply place the loop over the back of a chair and unwind carefully from there.

In projects where a good fit is essential, you must be careful when substituting yarn. Take time to check your tension carefully with the new yarn to obtain the finished size given in the pattern. However, one of the joys of crochet is how easy and fun it is to experiment with different yarn and hook sizes once you are more experienced. For projects like blankets and scarves, where the finished dimensions are flexible, throw caution to the wind and play with different weights, colours and types of yarn to obtain an exciting new look!

SUBSTITUTING YARNS

There are some fabulous yarns to choose from these days, so don't feel that you have to use the exact yarn or colour specified in a pattern. When substituting yarn, it is, however, important that you stick to the same weight of yarn. Otherwise the stitches will work at a different tension and the garment may come out the wrong size. The weight, for example DK, is usually stated on the ball band – if not check the needle/hook size suggested on the band.

The next factor you must take into consideration is the drape of the yarn suggested. You will get a very different looking fabric unless you use a similar fibre – for example heavy yarns such as cotton will hang very differently to a lofty, fluffy and light woollen yarn.

The stitch definition and colour choice are also important – there is no reason to crochet a complex stitch if the pattern does not show up well on the final garment. The most important tip is to always work a tension swatch (or four!) before you begin a project with a new yarn.

If you do decide to use a substitute yarn, consider the length of yarn in each ball. For example, if the pattern requires 10 balls of wool and each ball contains 120 metres of yarn, then the total amount used in the project is 1,200 metres. If the substitute yarn has only 80 metres per ball, you will need more than 10 balls.

To calculate how many more, divide the total length (1,200) by the substitute length (80) as follows:

1,200 ÷ 80 = 15 balls needed.

If in doubt, always buy a little extra.

CHOOSING HOOKS

When starting out, all you really need to know is that the thicker the yarn, the larger the hook you will need, and vice versa. With so many different designs of hooks available it is a good idea to try a few different types to find your favourite.

Traditional crochet hooks were made from thin steel, but today there are many different types of hooks to choose from. Made from a variety of materials and varying in shape, the type of hook you use will really come down to personal preference.

Bamboo/wooden hooks
Bamboo or wooden hooks come in many shapes and sizes. They can be carved to create handles that are more comfortable to grip. Often, unless they are lacquered or varnished, bamboo or wooden hooks can mean a less smooth hooking action. Look out for a sharp tip and deep hook, because shallow hooks can make grabbing the yarn more difficult.

Metal hooks
Any hooks with metal shafts are perfect for quick, smooth and easy hooking as they are unlikely to snag. Usually thinner hooks are made from steel for strength due to the stress that these hooks are subjected to. Aluminum hooks are similar to traditional steel hooks, but are lighter and not as cold to the touch.

Plastic hooks
Larger sized hooks usually come in plastic so they are light and easy to work with. They are often colour coordinated so you can see the correct size at a glance.

Handled hooks
Many modern hooks have some kind of grip along the shaft for comfort. The best of these have metal tips for smooth hooking action, but a handle made of plastic, wood or other material. This gives the crocheter more to hold on to, making for more comfortable crocheting and less stress on the hands.

Hook sizes
Hook sizes are determined by the thickness of their shaft, with their diameter usually increasing in increments of a millimetre or fractions of a millimetre. As a yarn increases in thickness, increase the size of the hook you use with it.

Hook sizes vary from country to country. When following the hooks recommended in a pattern, use this table to check which convention is being used.

CROCHET HOOK SIZES

Metric (mm)	UK	US	Metric (mm)	UK	*US
0.60		14	4	8	G/6
0.75		12	4.5	7	7
1		11	5	6	H/8
1.25		7	5.5	5	I/9
1.50		6	6	4	J/10
1.75		5	6.5	3	K/10½
2	14		7	2	
2.25		B/1	8	0	L/11
2.5	12		9	00	M/13
2.75		C/2	10	000	N/P/15
3	10		15		P/Q
3.25		D/3	16		Q
3.5	9	E/4	19		S
3.75		F/5			

* Letter or number may vary. Rely on the millimetre (mm) sizing.

BASIC TECHNIQUES

Once the basic stitches are mastered, almost anything can be created in crochet, and each of the following techniques is a variation on these simple stitches. Begin by achieving an even tension and practise by creating lengths of basic chain.

HOLDING THE HOOK AND YARN

In order to crochet competently, it is imperative that you hold the hook and yarn in a relaxed and comfortable fashion. This will also ensure that your tension is even and accurate throughout the project, which will in turn ensure that the stitches are worked more easily. There are two main ways of holding the hook and two main ways to tension the yarn in your fingers. You can choose whichever combination is natural for you, or use a variation of these, so long as your yarn is held evenly and you do not feel as if you are straining your fingers.

Practice is essential to discover your optimum hold, so try making lengths of chain until the action is produced naturally, almost without thinking, and the chains are even in size. It does not matter if your stitches tend to be slightly tight or even a little loose; you are aiming for an even tension throughout to achieve the most professional finish.

HOLDING THE HOOK

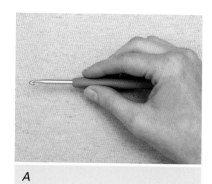

A

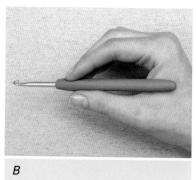

B

Knife Grip
Hold the hook in your dominant hand as you would a knife *(A)*.

Pencil Grip
Hold the hook in your dominant hand as you would a pencil *(B)*.

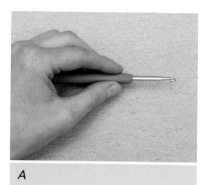

A

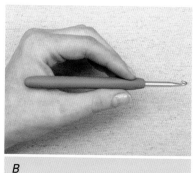

B

Working left-handed
Left-handers hold the hook in their left, dominant hand and the yarn in their right hand. This means that they crochet in the opposite direction to a right-hander, working from left to right instead of right to left and working clockwise instead of anti-clockwise when crocheting in the round.
To follow the directions in this book, hold a mirror to the pictures to show the altered direction of the stitches.

HOLDING THE YARN

Forefinger method

Wrap the ball end of the yarn around the little finger of the opposite hand, under the next two fingers and over the forefinger *(A)*. Hold the work steady with your middle finger and thumb, then when crocheting raise your forefinger to create tension *(B)*.

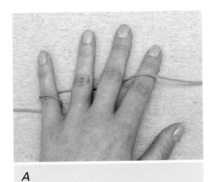
A

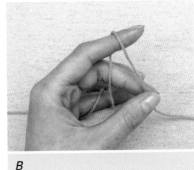
B

Middle finger method

Wrap the ball end of the yarn around the little finger of the opposite hand and over the other fingers *(A)*. Hold the work steady with your forefinger and thumb, then raise your middle finger when working to create tension *(B)*.

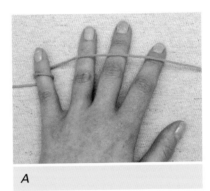
A

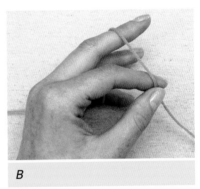
B

GETTING STARTED

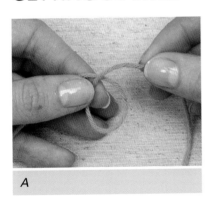
A

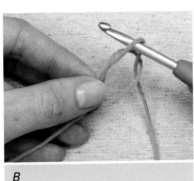
B

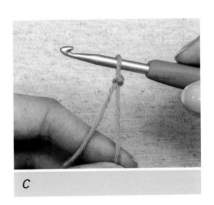
C

SLIPKNOT

A slipknot creates the first loop on the hook.

1. Make a loop in the yarn around 10–20 cm from the end *(A)*.

2. Insert the hook through the loop made, then pull a second loop of yarn through the first but do not pull the loose end of yarn through *(B)*. Pull on the ends of the yarn to draw up the knot to the hook, but do not pull too tightly or the hook will be hard to draw through the knot to make the first chain *(C)*.

CHAIN (ch)

Most crochet projects begin by making a length of chains, which the first row of stitches is then worked into.

Holding the hook with the point facing upwards in your dominant hand and the yarn in the other, grip the slipknot with the yarn holding hand. Work a yarn over hook (yoh) by passing the hook in front of the yarn, under and around it *(A)*.

1. Roll the hook towards you to catch the yarn and pull through loop on hook *(B)*. One chain made *(C)*.
2. Ensuring the stitches are even – not too loose or too tight – repeat to make a length of chain *(D)*.

The action of working the crochet stitches should create a constant rolling of the hook in your fingers; hold the hook pointing up when performing the yoh, then roll it towards you to point down when pulling through the loops on the hook so that you don't catch the hook in the stitches.

COUNTING A CHAIN

The right side of your chain is the one that looks like a little plait of 'v' shapes *(A)*. Each 'v' is a stitch and must be counted. When you are working the chain, you do not count the slipknot, but begin to count your chain when you pull through the first loop.

The back of the chain has little 'bumps'. Each bump is a stitch and should only be worked through if specifically indicated *(B)*.

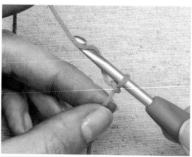

A

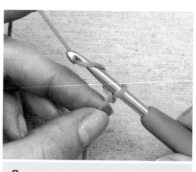

B

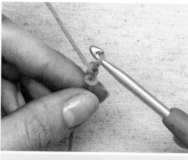

C

D

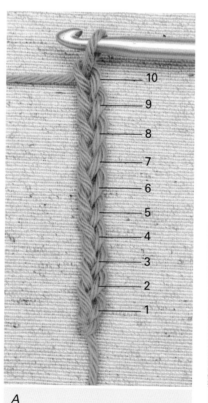

A

B

SLIP STITCH (ss/sl st)

A slip stitch is typically used to join one stitch to another or to join a stitch to another point. When used to join, it is usually made by picking up two strands of a stitch but when used all over, you generally only pick up the back loop.

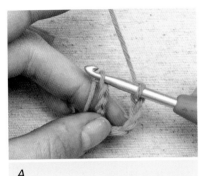

A

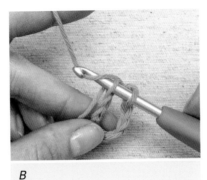

B

C

Insert hook into st or chain required *(A)*.

Yarn over hook, as when you make a chain *(B)*.

Pull a loop through all stitches/ loops/work on hook to finish and close the round *(C)*.

THE MAIN STITCHES

Once the yarn tension, hook hold and chain stitches have been mastered, you can progress onto the main stitches with confidence. These are all the techniques you will need to complete the projects in this book.

DOUBLE CROCHET (dc)

The shortest regular stitch, the double crochet (dc) is a crochet basic, used frequently to make a dense fabric that's perfect for amigurumi. When worked straight it is double-sided, so either side can be used as the right side.

TIP

Amigurumi is the Japanese art of knitting or crocheting small stuffed animals and anthropomorphic creatures. It has become popular all over the world.

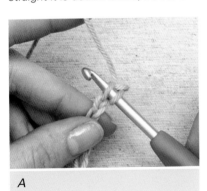

A

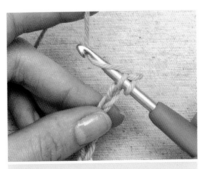

B

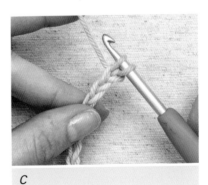

C

When working into the base chain, miss first chain and insert hook from front to back into second chain from hook *(A)*.

Grab the yarn held behind the work by placing hook under and around it – this is called yarn over hook (yoh) *(B)*.

Draw yarn through to front, two loops on hook *(C)*.

See overleaf

Double crochet continued

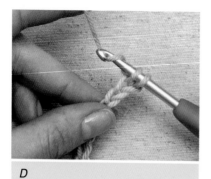

D

E

F

Yarn over hook as before *(D)*.

Draw through both loops to complete double crochet *(E)*.

Repeat these steps in each chain to the end, without missing out any further chains *(F)*.

G

H

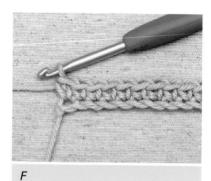

I

When the row is finished, turn the work so the reverse of the row just worked is facing you and work one chain to take you to the correct height for the next row. This is called a turning chain (t-ch) *(G)*.

On the next row, work a stitch in every stitch worked by inserting hook under the top two loops of each stitch from front to back *(H)*.

Complete stitch as before *(I)*.

HALF TREBLE CROCHET (htr)

The half treble (htr) is slightly taller than a double crochet stitch, with a softer drape to the resulting fabric. When worked straight it is double-sided, so either side can be used as the right side.

When working into the base chain, make a yarn over hook before inserting hook, miss first two chains and insert hook into third chain from hook. These two missed stitches count as the first half treble of the row *(A)*.

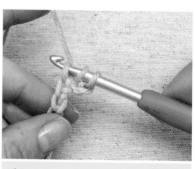

A

Yarn over hook again *(B)* and draw loop through base chain only. This creates three loops on the hook *(C)*.

Yarn over hook *(D)*. Draw yarn through three remaining loops on hook in one move to complete half treble *(E)*.

Repeat these actions in each chain to end, without missing out any further chains *(F)*.

When the row is finished, turn the work so the reverse of the row just worked is facing you and work two chains to get you to the height of the next row. The turning chain now counts as the first stitch of the row *(G)*.

On the next row, miss the first stitch, then work a stitch in next and every stitch of row by working a yarn over hook then inserting hook under the top two loops of each stitch from front to back *(H)*.

Complete stitch as before, by drawing a loop through, then drawing the yarn through all three loops at once *(I)*.

When you reach the end of the row, make sure you also work into the top chain of the turning chain.

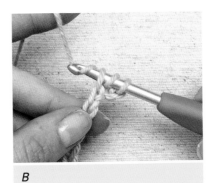

B

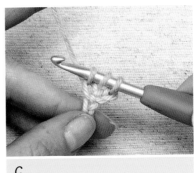

C

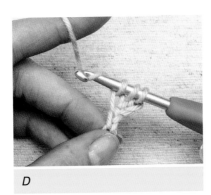

D

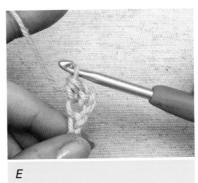

E

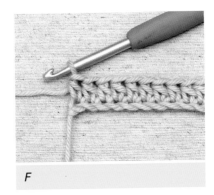

F

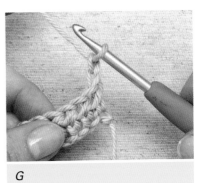

G

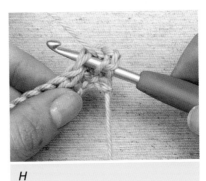

H

I

TREBLE CROCHET (tr)

The tallest of the basic stitches and perhaps the most commonly used, treble crochet (tr) is great for working up a fabric quickly and it is the most open of the three basic stitches. When worked straight it is double-sided, so either side can be used as the right side.

A

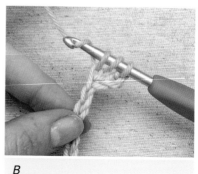

B

When working into the base chain, make a yarn over hook before inserting hook, miss the first three chains and insert hook into fourth chain from hook. These three missed stitches count as the first treble of the row *(A)*.

Yarn over hook again and draw loop through base chain only. This creates three loops on the hook. Yarn over hook *(B)*.

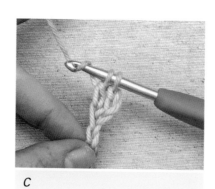

C

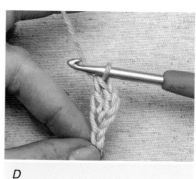

D

Draw yarn through two of the three remaining loops on hook, two loops remaining, yarn over hook once more *(C)*.

Draw through remaining two loops to complete the treble *(D)*.

Repeat these actions in each chain to end, without missing out any further chains *(E)*.

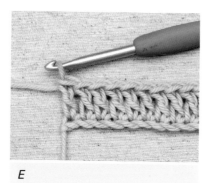

E

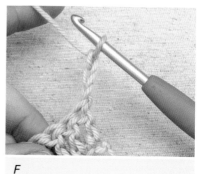

F

When the row is finished, turn the work so the reverse of the row just worked is facing you and work three chain stitches to get you to the height of the next row. This turning chain counts as the first stitch of the row *(F)*.

On the next row, miss the first stitch, then work a stitch in next and every stitch of row by working a yarn over hook then inserting hook under the top two loops of each stitch from front to back *(G)*.

G

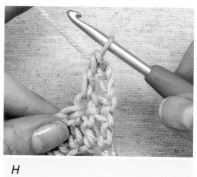

H

Complete stitch as before, by drawing a loop through, then working off the loops in groups of two as before *(H)*.

When you reach the end of the row, make sure you also work into the top chain of the turning chain *(I)*.

I

LESS COMMON STITCHES

DOUBLE TREBLE (dtr)

Each stitch following on from the treble crochet grows progressively taller in the same way as these stitches. This is achieved by adding more wraps of yarn around the hook before inserting it into the next stitch. To create the double treble, the yarn is wrapped around the hook twice before inserting, for a triple treble, the yarn is wrapped three times, and so on. Here, the double treble is demonstrated. Yarn around hook twice *(A)*.

Insert hook in next stitch, then draw a loop through. Four loops on hook *(B)*. Yarn around hook and draw through two loops, three loops on hook, yarn over hook *(C)*. Draw through two loops, two loops on hook, yarn around hook *(D)*. Draw through remaining two loops to complete stitch *(E)*. Each of the following stitches are worked in the same way, but the yarn is wrapped around the hook once more than the previous stitch before inserting into the fabric, then the loops are worked off in pairs *(F)*.

A

B

C

D

E

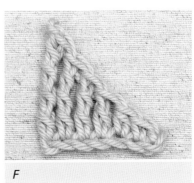

F

USING THE STITCHES

COUNTING STITCHES

When counting stitches *(below)*, you can count the top 'v' of each stitch, but it is easier to count each post or 'stem' of every stitch from the front of the fabric. Each post counts as one stitch. Remember that on a double crochet fabric, you do not count the turning chains but on the taller stitches, you do, unless the pattern instructs otherwise.

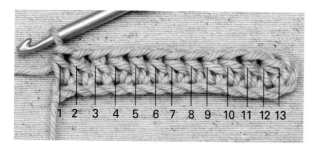

WHERE TO INSERT YOUR HOOK

The key to confident crocheting is knowing where to insert your hook. You can work into a stitch, between a stitch, into half of a stitch or even into a space or ring. Always check where the pattern indicates the stitches should be made.

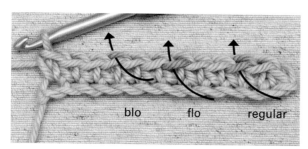

WORKING INTO DIFFERENT PARTS OF THE STITCH

All crochet stitches are always worked underneath both loops of the next stitch unless the pattern tells you otherwise. The top of the stitch looks like a 'v' lying along the top of the row of stitches *(above)*.

For regular working, insert hook under both loops of next stitch, then complete stitch.

Sometimes a pattern asks you to work only through one loop of the next stitch. To work through the front loop only (flo), insert hook under the front loop of next stitch, from the front to the centre of the stitch, then complete. To work through the back loop only (blo), insert hook through centre of stitch under the back loop to the back, then complete stitch.

Sometimes you are even asked to work in between the stitches. In these cases you ignore the top loops of the stitch and insert the hook between the posts of adjoining stitches.

WORKING STRAIGHT

When working straight you need to turn your work at the end of a row and then work a turning chain (t-ch) to the height of your intended stitch so that you can continue working along the next row *(below)*. This chain counts as the first stitch of the row and each stitch uses a different number of stitches depending on its height.

With half treble crochet and taller stitches, you miss the first stitch of the row, then work into every following stitch. This is because the turning chain is tall enough to count as the first stitch. This also means that you must work into the top of the turning chain from the previous row at the end of the row, treating it as the last stitch.

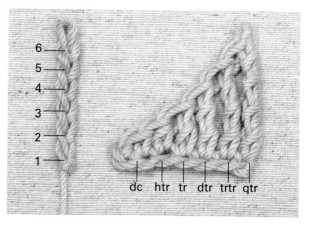

TALLER STITCHES

The triple treble (trtr) is worked as for the taller stitches, described on page 25, but the yarn is wrapped around hook three times before inserting. For the quadruple treble (qtr) the yarn is wrapped four times around the hook before inserting.

WORKING INTO A CHAIN

When working into a chain, you need to miss out the appropriate number of chain stitches called for with your particular stitch, then insert hook from front to back into next chain, under the top loop and if possible the back loop of the chain at the same time. You will have two loops above and one below the hook. Then complete the desired stitch.

WORKING INTO A SPACE

When the pattern instructs you to work into a chain space (ch-sp), insert your hook underneath the length of chain and into the space below.

KEEPING STRAIGHT EDGES

Knowing which stitch to work into when working straight can be a problem for most beginners. If you don't know which stitch to work into after making your turning chain, and want to make sure you work into the turning chain, which can easily be missed, try this tip:

When working the last stitch of the row insert a thread or stitch marker into that stitch *(A)*. Make your desired turning chain, placing a second (different colour), marker in the last chain *(B)*. On the following row, miss out the stitch with the first marker in, as your turning chain counts as the first stitch of the row *(C)*. Once you have worked across all stitches in the row, put a stitch into the marked chain, which is the top of the turning chain. Here, the turning chain has not yet been worked into – and if it was left off, the 'step' inwards this would create is obvious *(D)*.

A

B

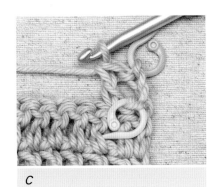

C

D

FASTEN OFF

When you have finished your fabric, you will need to secure the yarn so that the piece does not unravel. To do this: Pull up final loop of last stitch to make it bigger *(A)*, cut yarn, leaving enough of an end to weave in *(B)*. Pull short end through loop, drawing up tightly to secure.

A

B

HOW TO READ PATTERNS

Similar terms in the UK and US have different meanings, and this can cause confusion when following patterns if you do not know where the pattern was written. Ensure you check this before you begin.

This book is written using UK terminology. Below is a handy reference guide to the differences between the two sets of terms.

UK/Aus/Eur crochet terms	US crochet terms
(ss) slip stitch	(sl st/ss) slip stitch
(dc) double crochet	(sc) single crochet
(htr) half treble crochet	(hdc) half double crochet
(tr) treble crochet	(dc) double crochet
(dtr) double treble crochet	(tr) treble crochet
(trtr) triple treble crochet	(dtr) double treble crochet
miss	skip

All other crochet terms are the same in the UK and the US

READING PATTERNS

At first glance, patterns can seem like they're written in a foreign language. However, on closer inspection, you will notice that they are mainly composed of abbreviations and if you know what each of these is short for, you can read the pattern as you would a normal piece of writing. Try to familiarise yourself with the abbreviations shown on this page so you can follow the patterns in this book with confidence.

It may be helpful to read through a new pattern first, just to ensure that all the abbreviations and techniques used are familiar to you. This will save you having to look anything up during the making. However, sometimes looking ahead in the pattern is a hindrance because the pattern can seem so complicated it may put you off crocheting it.

Don't worry, though, when reading the pattern at the same time as hooking, most instructions become much clearer, and just by working through the instructions manually you will be able to understand what they mean as you progress.

The start of the pattern should include a summary of the materials, hooks and notions you will need to complete the pattern. It is a good idea to ensure you have gathered together all of these items before beginning. The text will name the brand of yarn used for the sample, its fibre content and how much of it you need. This book also gives you helpful tips for choosing an alternative yarn if you can't find the one suggested or want to use something different.

Special stitches should be outlined before the pattern starts, too. Ensure you familiarise yourself with these before beginning and if you have never tried the stitches before, it is a good idea to practise them first. This book includes step-by-step instructions for the most difficult of these stitches alongside the pattern text so that you can progress with confidence. Each pattern also outlines the basic stitches used right at the beginning of the text, so you can gauge whether the skill level is right for you.

TENSION/GAUGE

As we are not made like machines, every crocheter works in their own individual style and to their own individual tension, which makes it hard to gauge the resulting size and shape of a project without guidance. This is where a tension swatch comes in. The tension and measurements that a project is worked to are stated at the beginning of the pattern, to ensure you can create a finished piece in the size it is intended to be.

Before working a project, make a sample swatch in the desired yarn and using the suggested hook to see if your tension is the same as the one stated in the pattern. To do this, you need to crochet a small square of just over 10 x 10 cm in the main yarn and stitch used in the pattern, then count and calculate the average number of stitches the swatch has per centimetre. Hook a few more stitches and work more rows than the tension in the pattern suggests, as the edge stitches

tend to get a bit distorted so might give you the wrong result. When the swatch is completed, use a measuring tape or ruler to take some measurements. Count how many stitches and rows there are to 10 cm at different points over the swatch, then calculate the average to get your tension.

If you find you have more stitches per centimetre than indicated in the pattern, your tension is too tight and you need to work more loosely to ensure your project will come out at the right size. The best way to do this is to increase the size of hook you use by a quarter or half millimetre and hook the swatch again as many times as necessary until the tension is as close as you can get it. If there are fewer stitches than required then the tension is too loose, and you will need to decrease the size of hook and make more swatches in the same way until the tension is correct.

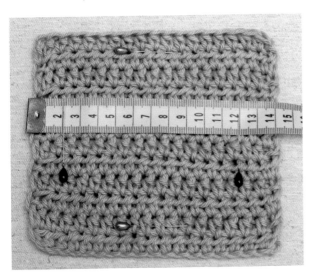

TIP
Don't worry if you can't get both the stitches and the rows to match exactly to the required tension. Simply concentrate on obtaining the correct number of stitches, as you can always work more or fewer rows as required in the pattern.

ABBREVIATIONS

beg	begin(s); beginning
bet	between
blo	back loop only
ch	chain
cl	cluster
cont	continue(s); continuing
dc	double crochet
dc2tog	double crochet two together (decrease one)
dec(s)	decrease(s); decreasing; decreased
dtr	double treble crochet
flo	front loop only
foll	follows; following
htr	half treble crochet
inc(s)	increase(s); increasing; increased
lp(s)	loop(s)
m	marker
patt(s)	pattern(s)
pm	place marker
rem	remain(s); remaining
rep(s)	repeat(s)
rnd(s)	round(s)
RS	right side
RSF	right side facing
ss	slip stitch
sp(s)	space(es)
st(s)	stitch(es)
t-ch	turning chain
tog	together
tr2tog	treble two together (decrease one)
tr	treble crochet
WS	wrong side
WSF	wrong side facing
yoh	yarn over hook

TIP

Label your tension swatches with the project description, yarn, stitch and hook used and file away neatly for future reference.

PATTERN TEXT

The instructions at the beginning of each row tell you whether you are working in rounds or rows, and which row or round you are working.
For example:

Row 1: *1ch, 1dc in each dc to end, turn.*

Rnd 1: *1ch, 1dc in each dc around, join rnd with ss.*
Watch out for the 'turn' command at the end of the row, which also indicates that you are working in rows as opposed to rounds.

There are a few symbols that are frequently used in crochet patterns to help you work out how to use the stitches. With brackets, work the instructions inside the brackets using the instructions directly outside the brackets for guidance. Brackets are used for a few different reasons. In this book, round brackets are used to indicate that a number of stitches are needed in one single stitch or space. For example:

Work (1tr, 1ch, 1tr) all in next stitch.
They are also used to denote different sizes. Where there are different sizes in a pattern, the smallest is listed, then all following ones are given inside brackets, increasing in size. This follows in the same way throughout the pattern, where a different instruction is needed for different sizes. It may be helpful where there are many different sizes to highlight all the instructions for your particular size first, by circling with a pencil. For example: *S (M, L).*

Square brackets are used to enclose instructions which need to be worked a number of times, with the number of repeats needed written outside the brackets. For example: *[Dc2tog, 4dc] twice.*

Sometimes an asterisk * will appear before certain parts of the pattern. This indicates that the instructions following the asterisk will be repeated within the same row.

STITCH COUNTS

In crochet, it is important to count your stitches as you work to ensure you have as many stitches in each row or round as the pattern indicates. This means that you can spot any mistakes easily. For ease of checking, this book includes stitch counts at the end of any row where an increase or decrease is made.

TIP
With crochet, you work the stitches either into a stitch, a chain, a chain space or a ring (st, ch, ch-sp). Read the instructions in a pattern carefully to see which is required.

PATTERN CHARTS

Crochet patterns often have an accompanying chart, which is a literal visual representation of the stitch pattern. You can use these charts in one of two ways – to follow the pattern entirely or to aid the understanding of the pattern. Even if you prefer to follow the text, a chart can still be a very good reference tool, as it represents quite accurately what the actual stitches look like, providing a reassuring visual guide to ensure that you are on the right track.

There are two key elements needed to understand a crochet chart: what each symbol means, and how the placement of that symbol shows where each stitch is worked into. The symbol key for all the stitches used in this book is shown here. Each symbol will be placed over the stitch or space you need to work the stitch into.

PATTERN CHART SYMBOLS

⟲	chain stitch (ch)
×	UK double crochet (dc) US single crochet (sc)
T	UK half treble crochet (htr) US half double crochet (hdc)
⊤	UK treble crochet (tr) US double crochet (dc)
∨	UK 2 double crochet in 1 stitch (2dc) US 2 single crochet in 1 stitch (2sc)
↓	UK 3 double crochet in 1 stitch (3dc) US 3 single crochet in 1 stitch (3sc)
●	UK slip stitch (ss) US slip stitch (sl st/ss)
⌒	stitch above the symbol is worked in back loop only
	v-stitch
	shell stitch
	bobble stitch

FURTHER TECHNIQUES

Crochet is perfect for creating seamless three-dimensional shapes as it can easily be worked in the round, with stitches adding to the sculptural appearance. The skills learned here will be especially useful for making decorative objects such as baskets.

WORKING IN THE ROUND

When working in the round, instead of working backwards and forwards along the work, turning at each end, you simply work with the right side facing you at all times and do not turn.

To begin working in the round, you most often start one of three ways, each of which creates a different centre to the first round of stitches.

WORKING AROUND A RING

This is the most common method of working in the round and it creates a large hole at the centre of your work, with its size dependent on the length of chain used originally.

Make a length of chain as required, then instead of working back along the chain, insert hook into the first chain stitch made.

Yarn over hook and work a slip stitch to join, by drawing

A

B

C

D

E

F

yarn through everything on hook *(A)*. This creates a ring *(B)*.
Work your turning chain dependent on which stitch you will be
working into the ring. Insert hook into the centre of the ring from
front to back *(C)*.
Draw yarn through to the front of the ring *(D)*.
Complete first stitch into this ring – here a double crochet is shown *(E)*.
Work required number of stitches into the centre of the ring *(F)*, then
join round with a slip stitch to the first stitch made in the ring *(G)*.
Do not turn, but continue the next row around the last.

G

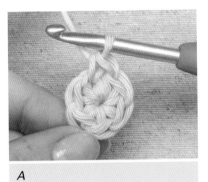

A

B

C

D

WORKING IN SPIRALS

Sometimes when working in
double crochet in the round, as they
are so short, it is easier to work
in spirals without turning chains
or joining each round. To work in
spirals, simply place a marker at the
beginning of the round to denote
where you are working to each
round. At the end of the first round,
do not join with a slip stitch (ss), but
simply work a double crochet into
the first stitch of round *(A)*.

Place marker in this stitch to
mark where the round starts *(B)*.
Continue in pattern to the end of
round *(C)*.
Remove marker and work into first
stitch of round.
Place marker in first stitch and
repeat *(D)*.

ADJUSTABLE RING

This method is also referred to
as the magic loop or magic ring,
so-called as it creates a round with
no hole at the centre. Here it is
demonstrated with double crochet.

Make a loop in your yarn, at least
15 cm from tail end *(A)*. Insert hook
through loop from front to back *(B)*.

See overleaf

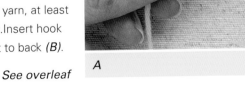

A

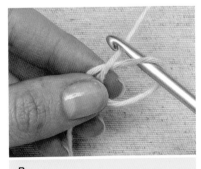

B

Adjustable ring continued

Pull loop though to front of ring, make 1 chain stitch (1ch) to secure *(C)* and then complete a double crochet around the loop and the tail end of yarn held double *(D)*.

Work all following stitches into the ring in the same way, over both strands of yarn in the ring *(E)*.

Once all stitches have been worked, pull the loose tail end of yarn to close the ring *(F)* and join round with a slip stitch to the first stitch made.

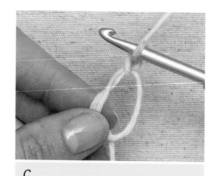

C

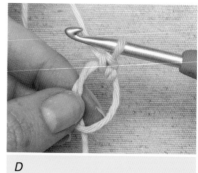

D

E

F

WORKING INTO A SHORT CHAIN

You can create a smaller hole in the centre of your work by working into a chain as few as 2ch in length.

For **double crochet (dc)**, as in this example, work 2 chain stitches (2ch) *(A)*. (For **half treble crochet** [htr] you would work 3ch and for trebles, 4ch).

Insert hook into the first chain and work first stitch into this chain *(B)*.

Now work required number of stitches into the same chain *(C)*.

The sheer amount of stitches worked into one place will cause them to fan out into a round. Join this round with a slip stitch to the first stitch made in the ring *(D)*.

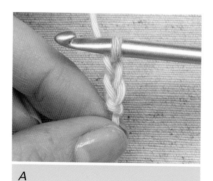

A

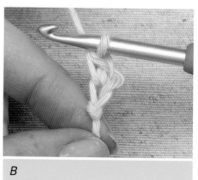

B

C

D

STRIPING

Working a stripe in crochet uses the same joining technique as adding in a new ball of the same colour. It is very easy to do and yet creates striking results, so it is a handy technique for the beginner crocheter to learn. There are a few ways of joining in a new yarn in crochet, and each will create a different finish. You can stick to the method you find easiest, or pick the best technique each time for the pattern you are using.

TIP

When joining in a new ball of the same colour, work as for a stripe, adding in the new ball in the last step of a stitch. Try to join the new ball at the beginning of the row where possible as it is easier to hide the yarn ends.

To make a simple slip stitch join, fasten off the old yarn, then hold the new yarn at the back of work. Insert the hook into the next stitch, chain or chain space, grab the new yarn from the back of the work *(A)* and draw a loop through to the front of the work. Make one chain to secure, then continue in pattern *(B)*.

A

B

For a neater join, you can also join in the final step of the previous row. Work the final stitch of previous row to the final step, so that the stitch is unfinished. Draw new colour through the remaining loops on your hook, completing the stitch and joining the new colour at the same time.

Here you can see how to work a new colour over double crochet *(C)* and how to work a new colour over treble crochet *(D)*.

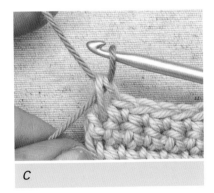

C

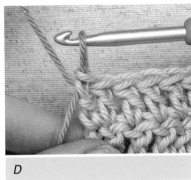

D

WEAVING ENDS AS YOU GO

To save time when finishing your work, you can also weave in your ends as you go by crocheting over both short ends as you stitch, rather than having to do so at the end.

Simply hold both pieces of yarn over the stitch along the next row and work over them as you work into the stitches *(A)*.

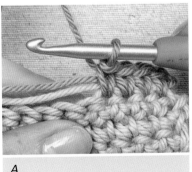

A

SHAPING

Making planned increases and decreases to shape your work can take your crochet to the next level by creating three dimensional shapes and complicated looking patterns. You can increase and decrease anywhere along a row or round and you can decrease more than one stitch at once.

INCREASING

To work an extra stitch, you simply need to work into the same stitch more than once. Here, double crochet is used to demonstrate increasing in the middle of the row. Work one stitch as normal. Insert hook into same stitch as one just worked and complete stitch. One stitch increased *(A)*.

When working a taller stitch such as a half treble or a treble, you work in the same way as the double crochet. However, at the beginning of the round, to increase one stitch, simply work into the stitch you usually miss. Work your turning chain as normal, then yarn over hook and insert into the first stitch of the round, at the bottom of the turning chain. Complete treble as normal *(B)*.

TIP
Knowing how to manipulate the shape of your crochet by increasing or decreasing the number of stitches is helpful when altering patterns to achieve the best fit.

A

B

DECREASING

Method one

When decreasing in crochet, the easiest method is to simply miss out a stitch. Work to where indicated in the pattern, miss next stitch, insert hook in following stitch *(A)*. Complete next stitch as normal, one stitch decreased *(B)*.

When working a double crochet stitch, as in the example, this technique creates a neat decrease, however in some stitch patterns it creates a more noticeable hole where the missed stitch lies. Sometimes this is desirable, as in lace patterns, but for a seamless decrease, work method two, which is a technique that uses half finished stitches that are then joined together.

Method two

This technique uses half finished stitches, which are then joined.

DECREASING DOUBLE CROCHET

Insert hook into next stitch, yarn over hook and draw a loop through the stitch, but do not finish the double crochet stitch as usual. Two loops on hook *(A)*.

A

B

A

Insert hook into following stitch, yarn over hook and draw a loop through the next stitch, three loops on hook in total. Yarn over hook *(B)* draw loop through all loops on hook, drawing two stitches together. One stitch decreased *(C)*.

B

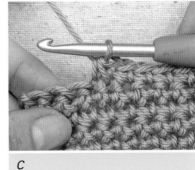

C

DECREASING HALF TREBLE CROCHET

Work yarn over hook, insert into next stitch and draw a loop through, three loops on hook *(A)*. Repeat into the following stitch, five loops on hook *(B)*. Yarn over hook, draw yarn through all five loops on hook to draw the two half trebles together. One stitch decreased *(C)*.

A

B

C

DECREASING TREBLE CROCHET

Work a treble into the next stitch until the last step of the stitch, two loops on hook *(A)*. Do the same into the following stitch, three loops on hook. Yarn over hook *(B)*. Draw yarn through all three loops on hook to draw the two trebles together. One stitch decreased *(C)*.

A

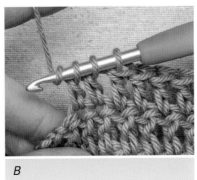

B

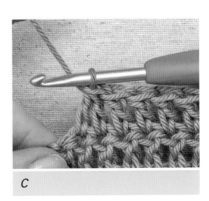

C

FINISHING

Rushing the final execution of a project may result in a sloppy finish which can ruin the overall look of your crochet, so do master these handy techniques to ensure a professional result every time.

BLOCKING

The blocking of crochet is the action of stretching or manipulating the final pieces into their correct shape. Blocking can help to turn a project from ordinary or misshapen to practically perfect in every way. This manipulation can be achieved using a few different techniques, depending on the project. For example, lace crochet needs a more stringent wet blocking to allow the lace to 'bloom' or open up to show off the lacy pattern. Wearable projects will need some steam blocking to set the stitches and create a more fluid drape to the fabric, while more structural projects like baskets won't need blocking at all, as they need to retain some stiffness.

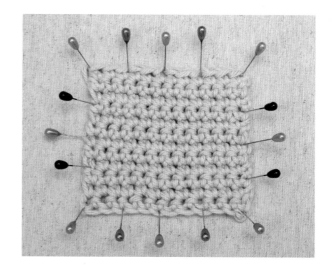

Blocking must always be done prior to sewing up the pieces, to ensure all are the correct size and prevent the final item becoming misshapen once sewn together. Tension swatches must always be treated in the same way that the final project will be, so ensure they are blocked to the same degree as the planned project, to ensure you obtain the correct measurements.

crochet before steaming, remembering not to press too hard with the iron. If using a cloth, remove it once you have steamed the piece but do not unpin until the pieces are completely cooled and dry. If you wish to ensure two identical pieces are the exact same size and shape, pin them on top of each other as a guide and then work the block as above.

STEAM BLOCK

Basic pieces can sometimes be simply pinned to shape and then lightly steamed with an iron set to 'steam shot' to set the stitches. When pinning, be careful not to overstretch the edges, and use plenty of pins to prevent uneven, scalloped edges. A word of warning; do not press with the iron, as this will flatten the stitches, simply hover the iron over the fabric and allow the steam to work its magic. You can also try spritzing a little water over the piece if you wish to ensure a stronger block, or alternatively lay a slightly damp cloth over the

WET BLOCK

With lace and with any piece that has, for some reason, been worked to the wrong measurements, you must block the pieces carefully. You can buy specialist blocking wires, especially good for large lace pieces such as shawls or scarves, but you can also achieve the same effect by pinning to a towel or to your ironing board. To wet block, thoroughly dampen the crochet carefully by submerging in cool water and a wool wash if desired. Take out of the water carefully and remove excess water by laying the fabric out flat on a towel. Roll up the towel and press firmly on the resulting sausage shape until all the surplus is squeezed gently into the towel.

Pin out gently into the correct shape onto a towel or blocking mat as with a steam block and leave to dry completely before removing pins.

JOINING CROCHET

Crochet is really quite fabulous and flexible as there is a myriad of different ways to join your fabric, not just by sewing two pieces together, but by crocheting them together. Not only can you crochet pieces together, but you can join the pieces as you go with slip stitches on the last round, meaning that when you have finished crocheting your fabric, the piece is already joined.

SLIP STITCH JOIN

A

B

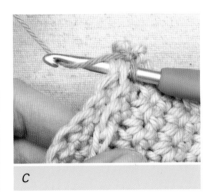

C

The wonderful thing about crochet is that if you do not like sewing, you needn't use a needle at all. A crochet join is neat and quick to work.

Simply arrange your pieces with right sides facing each other, as if you were to sew them together, then attach your yarn to the right-hand end of the edge to be joined and work a row of slip stitch all along the edge, through both sides of the fabric at the same time.

Insert hook into first set of adjoining stitches from front and back pieces. You can either work just through the back loops of each stitch *(A)* or through the whole stitch of each fabric for a thicker seam *(B)*.

Yarn over hook, draw through all stitches and loops on hook to complete first slip stitch *(C)*. Repeat along seam, working into every set of stitches.

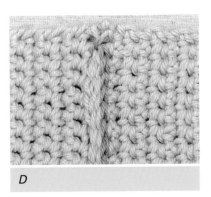

D

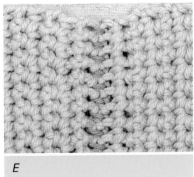

E

Here you can see what the seam looks like from the right side *(D)* and the wrong side *(E)*. Either side of the seam can be used as the right side, choose your favourite.

DOUBLE CROCHET JOIN

Work as for slip stitch join, but working a double crochet into each stitch instead of a slip stitch.

Insert hook into first set of adjoining stitches from front and back pieces as for the slip stitch join. Yarn over hook, draw through both stitches to front, yarn over hook *(A)*, and draw through both loops, double crochet complete *(B)*.

Repeat along seam, working into every set of stitches.

Here you can see what the seam looks like from the right side *(C)* and the wrong side *(D)*. Either side of the seam can be used as the right side, choose your favourite.

A

B

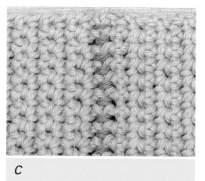
C

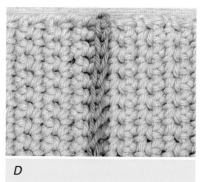
D

WEAVING IN ENDS

If you haven't hidden your ends by weaving as you go, you must secure them at the end of your project for a neat finish and to ensure the work does not unravel. Leave all your yarn tails long – at least 15–20 cm – so you have plenty of yarn to work with.

Thread the yarn end onto a yarn needle and weave yarn along the stitches of the last row at the back of the fabric for at least 5 cm *(A)*. Then thread back under several stitches in the opposite direction to ensure the security of the yarn *(B)*.

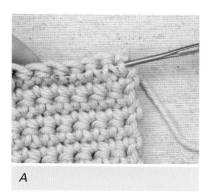
A

B

TIP

If your project will have to be sewn up, leave extra long tail ends and don't weave them in until the seams are sewn, as the ends can be used to sew up the seams. Or, if they are not actually needed to sew up the seams, you can simply weave them neatly into the seams so that they won't show on the right side of the work.

DECORATIVE EDGINGS

If you do find that despite all your efforts, the sides of your fabric are less than perfect, don't worry – edge them! Even a simple row of double crochet will neaten any border.

If you intend to work a decorative border, you should always work a double crochet row first for neatness, making sure the double crochet row has the correct multiple of stitches for the edging you intend to work. For neatness, even if the border is going to be a contrasting colour to the main fabric, work the double crochet foundation row in the same colour as the fabric, and then change colour for the decorative edge.

To keep your edging even, work a double crochet into every stitch along the top of the fabric, then work as evenly as you can along the sides of the rows and work a stitch into every chain along the bottom edge. The size of the stitch will determine how many stitches

you work along the side. A double crochet should have one stitch worked for every row, with the number of stitches worked into each row increasing with the stitch height, although this may change depending on the yarn and hook you use, so take care.

Beware of adding too many stitches as your edge will buckle, too few and it will draw in. If in doubt, rip back the edge and try again!

When you get to the corner, insert three stitches into the corner stitch to turn it *(A)*, and then use the central stitch of the three as the corner stitch in each following round.

Here you can see the finished edge of a double crochet worked evenly in a contrasting colour to demonstrate the technique *(B)*, but when working the edge, it is better to use the same colour as the fabric for the neatest finish. Work a second or multiple rounds off this neat base edge for a more embellished finish.

A

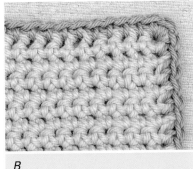

B

TIP

A wide variety of patterns are available for decorative borders and trims. Once you have mastered the basic edging technique, it will be possible to embellish it to create beautifully intricate trims.

WASHING AND CARE ESSENTIALS

When crocheted in a quality yarn and cared for in the correct manner, hand-made products can last for many years. It is sensible to file the ball band from your project somewhere secure so that you can refer to it when you need to launder the fabric. Before making any decisions about how to care for an item, always check the ball band for as much information as possible.

Avoid using biological washing powders or those with any kind of added brighteners. Soap flakes or a specialist no-rinse wool wash are best.

Make sure the water is cool and the detergent is completely dissolved. If the detergent needs warm or

hot water in order to disperse thoroughly, make sure it has had time to cool before you begin. Do not wring, twist, or rub the fabric, and wash the project as quickly as possible.

To remove most of the water from your garment, lay it out flat on a towel, roll up the towel and press firmly on the resulting sausage shape until all the excess is squeezed gently into the towel.

Never hang your hand made items to dry as they will stretch, sometimes to ridiculous lengths. When drying, block by laying it out on a clean, dry towel and pin lightly to size, as with blocking (see pages 38–39) if the piece needs to be reshaped.

GROUPED STITCHES

Working multiple crochet stitches into the same space produces beautiful textures. The most basic type of group is an increase. However, despite consisting of more than one stitch, the stitches shown here are generally counted as a single stitch.

SHELLS

One of the prettiest ways to enhance a group of stitches is to put five or more stitches into the same space or stitch. This is usually called a shell and they generally consist of taller stitches such as trebles. A basic shell will usually be made of five trebles, *(A)* or an odd number of stitches, so that on the next row you can work into the centre treble only *(B)*. Due to the size of the shell, you usually miss stitches either side of a

A

B

shell when working the first row to give it space and prevent buckling of the fabric.

CLUSTERS

Clusters are groups of stitches worked into the same stitch, and then decreased again quickly to create three-dimensional texture. Clusters can be confusing to work so here is an outline of the differences in working the main cluster stitches: bobbles, popcorns and puffs.

Bobbles

A bobble is a number of stitches (generally trebles) all half finished and all worked into the same stitch. Once the desired number of half-finished trebles have been completed, all loops are decreased to finish the stitches and complete the bobble.

Work six trebles to the last step, all into the next stitch, seven loops on hook, *(A)* yarn over hook, draw yarn through all loops on hook to complete bobble *(B)*.

A

B

Popcorns

Popcorns are a number of complete stitches worked into one stitch, as with a shell. Once completed, they are reduced down to create a striking three-dimensional stitch. Work five trebles into the next stitch *(A)*. Pull up on loop on hook to elongate *(B)*. Remove hook from loop and insert into first of five trebles *(C)*. Insert hook back into long loop and tighten it up, yarn round hook *(D)*. Draw yarn through everything on hook, one popcorn made *(E)*.

A

B

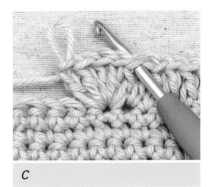

C

D

E

Puffs

A puff is a number of elongated half trebles worked into the same stitch, then finished together like a bobble. Yarn round hook, insert into next stitch, draw a loop through stitch and pull it up to the height of all other stitches in the row *(A)*. Yarn round hook, insert into same stitch, pull a loop through stitch and pull it up to the height of all other stitches in the row. Repeat desired number of times, here four half finished half trebles have been worked, nine loops on hook in total *(B)*. Yarn round hook and draw through all loops on hook. One puff made *(C)*.

A

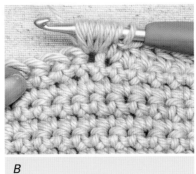

B

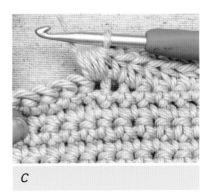

C

GETTING STARTED

Here you'll find an exciting selection of projects that you can crochet very simply. Some of them, such as the Pom-Pom Bookmarks, are so quick to make that you will want to create them in a whole host of colours. Even the larger-scale projects are easy to achieve - the super-cool granny squares blanket, for example, is constructed from lots of simple-to-make crochet squares.

Pom-Pom
BOOKMARKS

This is a simple and fun way to mark a page! It is always good to practise the very basic stitches as much as possible, and this project is perfect for using all those small samples you have made.

MATERIALS

Any weight or colour of yarn can be used.
Here we have used Patons™ Merino Extrafine DK,
*   100% wool, 50 g/120 m per ball.*
Small amounts of each colour:
*   Yarn A: 0121 'Canary'*
*   Yarn B: 0134 'Coral'*
*   Yarn C: 0135 'Pale Pink'*
*   Yarn D: 0167 'Mint'*
*   Yarn E: 0169 'Teal'*
*   Yarn F: 0192 'Medium Grey Heather'*
4 mm hook
Yarn needle
Pom-pom maker

YARN ALTERNATIVES

*Any weight of yarn will work here, the bookmarks
will simply differ in size depending on the yarn used.
Ensure you choose a yarn hairy enough to make fluffy,
plump pom-poms.*

STITCH TECHNIQUES

Chain (ch)
Double crochet (dc)
Half treble crochet (htr)
Treble crochet (tr)
Working straight
Double crochet edge
Pom-poms

GENERAL TIPS

❖ *Practise the simple stitches by creating a very basic
strip, then attach a pom-pom to the top.*

TENSION

Exact tension is not essential for this pattern.

FINISHED MEASUREMENTS

*Each bookmark is approx 3 cm wide and 15 cm long,
not including the pom-pom.*
The pom-poms shown are 6 cm in diameter.

PATTERN

There are three different bookmark patterns depending
on which stitch needs practice.

Double crochet bookmark

With 4 mm hook and desired shade, make 31ch.
Row 1: 1dc in second ch from hook and each ch to end,
turn (30dc).
Rows 2–4: 1ch, 1dc in each st to end, turn.
Edging: 1ch, 1dc in each st to last st, (1dc, 1ch, 1dc) in
last st for corner. *(A)*
Without turning work, *continue down next side of
bookmark, working evenly in dc to next corner, (1dc,
1ch, 1dc) in corner; rep from * to end, join rnd with ss
to first dc.
Fasten off yarn and weave in all ends.

A

Half treble crochet bookmark

With 4 mm hook and desired shade, make 32ch.

Row 1: 1htr in third ch from hook and each ch to end, turn – 30htr.

Rows 2 & 3: 2ch, 1htr in each st to end, turn.

Edging: Work as for double crochet bookmark. Fasten off yarn and weave in all ends.

Treble crochet bookmark

With 4 mm hook and desired shade, make 33ch.

Row 1: 1tr in fourth ch from hook and each ch to end, turn – 30tr.

Row 2: 3ch, 1tr in each st to end, turn.

Edging: Work as for double crochet bookmark. Fasten off yarn and weave in all ends.

Pin out and block all bookmarks to shape.

FINISHING

Make a 6 cm diameter pom-pom and sew to one end of the bookmark.

HOW TO USE A POM-POM MAKER

Wind yarn around each half of the pom-pom maker *(A)*.
Close the two halves together to make a complete
circle and carefully cut around the outside edge of
the yarn circle *(B)*.

Tie a piece of yarn approximately 30 cm long very tightly
around the middle of the pom-pom. Knot tightly to
secure *(C)*.

Carefully pull the pom-pom maker apart to release the
pom-pom *(D)*.

Neaten the pom-pom by cutting off any yarn ends
that are too long and then fluff up into a neat, squishy
sphere by rolling gently between your hands *(E)*.

A

B

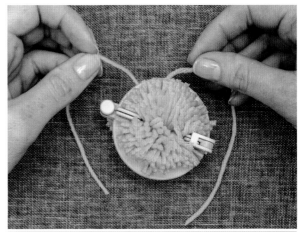

C

D

E

Pretty
PICOT EDGING

Crochet edging works really well alongside other fabrics. Here a simple picot edge adds a pretty contrast to a plain shirt collar.

MATERIALS

You will need a fine crochet thread in any colour.
Here we have used Bergère De France™ Coton Fifty,
50% acrylic, 50% cotton, 50 g/140 m per ball.

Shade: 24419 'Nectarine' x 1 ball

White shirt with collar

2.25 mm hook

Sewing needle with big enough eye to fit the yarn
through

Yarn needle

YARN ALTERNATIVES

Any fine crochet thread may be substituted.

STITCH TECHNIQUES

Chain (ch)

Double crochet (dc)

Picot

Blanket stitch – sewing

(See also Special Stitches)

GENERAL TIPS

This edging is worked from a blanket stitch base
and can be crocheted around any fabric edge that is
prepared with a blanket stitch. A bold edge is a very
modern way of using the technique to customise the
hems, cuffs and collars of plain garments.

TENSION

Exact tension is not essential for this pattern.

SPECIAL STITCHES

Picot: 3ch, ss in bottom of chain.

Blanket Stitch (sewing): To begin the blanket stitch,
insert the needle from back to front of fabric, 1 cm
from the edge. Bring the needle over the edge and
back through the fabric from the back in the same
place as before, creating a loop around the edge. (A)
Insert the needle sideways through the loop just
made at the edge of the fabric to anchor thread (B).
*Insert the needle from front to back through the
fabric 1 cm along from previous stitch and 1 cm down
from the edge. Bring the needle up to the front around
the edge and through loop made (C).

Pull the stitch tight. Repeat from * for each subsequent
blanket stitch (C).

PATTERN

Prepare the edge to be embellished by working a
blanket stitch all around the Right Side (RS) of the
edge, using the yarn in which edging will be worked.
Ensure the blanket stitches are approximately
1 cm apart.

With 2 mm hook and Right Side Facing (RSF), attach
yarn to the first blanket stitch with ss.

Edge Row: (2dc, picot [see Special Stitches], 1dc) in
top part of each blanket stitch around edge.
Fasten off and weave in all ends.

A

B

C

Simple STRIPED SCARF

A striped scarf is a perfect first wearable project for beginners. A long strip is so simple to make – there is plenty of length for practising changing colour and maintaining neat, straight edges, plus it is fabulously stylish and practical.

MATERIALS

You will need an Aran/worsted weight yarn in five colours.

Here we have used Scheepjes™ Stone Washed XL, 70% cotton, 30% acrylic, 50 g/75 m per ball.

Yarn A: 854 'Crystal Quartz' x 2 balls

Yarn B: 856 'Coral' x 1 ball

Yarn C: 842 'Smokey Quartz' x 2 balls

Yarn D: 853 'Amazonite' x 2 balls

Yarn E: 855 'Green Agate' x 1 ball

6 mm hook

Yarn needle

TENSION

Work 13htr and 10 rows to measure 10 x 10 cm using a 6 mm hook or the size needed to achieve the correct tension.

FINISHED MEASUREMENTS

Scarf is approx 25 x 180 cm.

PATTERN NOTES

❖ *Change the colour on the last step of the last stitch of the previous row.*

❖ *On the row before the colour change, work to the last step of the last stitch of the row. Three loops on the hook.*

❖ *Draw the new colour through all the loops on the hook.*

YARN ALTERNATIVES

When substituting yarn, the required lengths will vary from one brand of yarn to another. Any Aran/worsted weight yarn will substitute here, although experimenting with yarn weights and hook sizes will simply cause the scarf to come out bigger or smaller.

STITCH TECHNIQUES

Chain (ch)

Half treble crochet (htr)

Working straight

Striping

Weaving in ends as you go

Double crochet edge

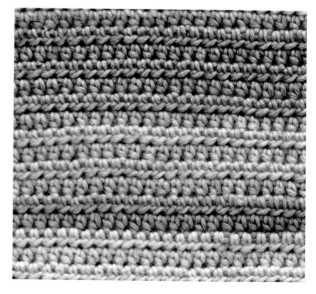

❖ Turn and make 2ch for the turning chain, then continue along the row in the new colour. Colour change completed.

❖ Weave in the yarn ends as you go, if desired. Hold the yarn ends along the top of the stitches of the last row and work all the stitches of the next row around the yarn ends, trapping them inside the stitch.

❖ The scarf shown was randomly striped using the colours stated. If even stripes are desired please note that the sample shown measures 25 x 180 cm and used 350 g/525 m in total of Scheepjes™ Stone Washed XL, which weighs 50 g per ball. Bear in mind more yarn may be needed for a longer scarf. If you want to work a plain scarf you will only need 7 balls.

❖ Because the stripes are of different sizes, not all balls may be used completely. Simply crochet until the desired length of scarf is reached.

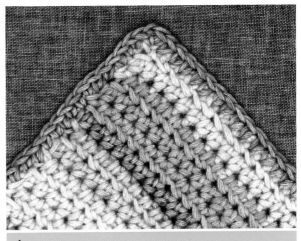

A

PATTERN

With 6 mm hook and desired shade, make 33ch.

Row 1: 1htr in third ch from hook and each ch to end, turn – 31htr.

Row 2: 2ch (counts as htr), 1htr in each st to end, turn – 31htr.

Rep last row until scarf measures 180 cm or desired length, striping randomly throughout.

Fasten off yarn.

Edging

Join yarn C to any edge with a ss.

Edging row: 1ch, work evenly in dc around entire edge of scarf, placing (1dc, 1ch, 1dc) in each corner, join rnd with ss to first dc *(A)*.

Fasten off yarn.

FINISHING

Weave in any remaining ends and block lightly to shape.

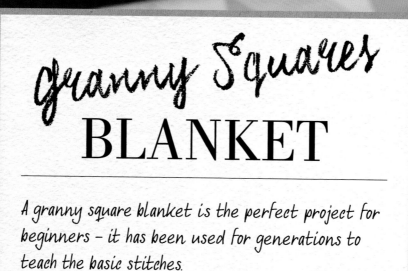

granny Squares
BLANKET

A granny square blanket is the perfect project for beginners – it has been used for generations to teach the basic stitches.

MATERIALS

You will need an Aran/worsted weight yarn in
five colours.
Here we have used MillaMia™ Naturally Soft Aran,
100% Extra Fine Merino wool, 50 g/80 m per ball.
  Yarn A: 202 'Stone' x 9 balls
  Yarn B: 201 'Cinder' x 3 balls
  Yarn C: 240 'Ochre' x 2 balls
  Yarn D: 221 'Ivory' x 2 balls
  Yarn E: 200 'Slate' x 1 ball
5 mm hook
Yarn needle

YARN ALTERNATIVES

When substituting yarn, the required lengths will vary
from one brand of yarn to another. Any Aran/worsted
weight yarn will substitute here, although experimenting
with yarn weights and hook sizes will simply cause the
blanket to come out bigger or smaller. Blanket uses a
total weight of 700 g.

STITCH TECHNIQUES

Chain (ch)
Treble crochet (tr)
Working in the round
Striping
Joining motifs as you go
Granny pattern edge

GENERAL TIPS

❖ *Granny motifs are a traditional and very familiar*
crochet technique, but by playing with a monochrome
colour palette and adding a pop of colour, the
conventional pattern is given a stunning contemporary
update to create this gorgeous blanket.

TENSION

One granny square measures approx 10 x 10 cm
using a 5 mm hook or the size needed to achieve
the correct tension.

FINISHED MEASUREMENTS

Blanket measures approx 100 x 100 cm.

PATTERN NOTES

❖ *This blanket uses 81 motifs, and you can make it*
bigger or smaller by adding or subtracting motifs – the
edging is still worked in the same way.
❖ *Play with the colours as you wish. This blanket uses*
41 motifs with a yarn B centre, then with a random
mix of the shades C-E as the central colour for the
remaining 40 motifs.

PATTERN

Granny motif

With 5 mm hook and any desired shade apart from yarn
A, make 4ch, join with a ss to form a ring.
Rnd 1: 3ch (counts as first tr here and throughout), 2tr
in ring, 3ch, [3tr in ring, 3ch] twice more. Join rnd with
ss to top of first ch.
Fasten off yarn.

A

B

C

Attach yarn A to any corner sp of Rnd 1.

Rnd 2: 3ch, (2tr, 3ch, 3tr) in same sp, 1ch, *(3tr, 3ch, 3tr) in next 3ch-sp, 1ch; rep from * twice more. Join rnd with ss to top of first ch.

Rnd 3: Ss to next ch-sp, 3ch, (2tr, 3ch, 3tr) in same sp, 1ch, 3tr in next 1ch-sp, 1ch, *(3tr, 3ch, 3tr) in next 3ch-sp for corner, 1ch, 3tr in next 1ch-sp, 1ch; rep from * around. Join rnd with ss to top of first ch.

Work first motif complete to Rnd 3. Work all following motifs to Rnd 2, then join to last motif made while working Rnd 3 as follows:

Join as you go Rnd 3:

Ss to next ch-sp, 3ch, (2tr, 3ch, 3tr) in same sp, 1ch, 3tr in next 1ch-sp, 1ch, 3tr in corner sp, 1ch *(A)*.

Slip stitch into the corresponding corner chain of the previous motif *(B)*.

Complete the corner stitch of the second motif by working one more chain, then work the next 3tr group of the corner *(C)*.

Now work a slip stitch into the next corresponding

1ch-sp of the first motif (which counts as the usual 1ch) *(D)*.

Now complete the next 3tr group into the next 1ch-sp of the working motif as usual *(E)*.

Work a slip stitch into the next corresponding 1ch-sp of the first motif (which counts as the usual 1ch).

Now working into the second corner, work (3tr, 1ch) into the corner ch-sp, then slip stitch into the corresponding corner chain of the previous motif *(F)*.

Complete the corner as before, one side is now joined to the previous motif *(G)*.

For motifs that need only be joined along one side, continue around the rest of the round as per Rnd 3 *(H)*.

For motifs that need to be joined along two sides, continue along the next side, joining at each 1ch-sp and the centre ch of each corner to the corresponding motif's ch-sps as the first side, then complete Rnd 3 as normal *(I)*.

Make 81 motifs, joining each to the last in a square, 9 motifs wide by 9 motifs tall. Position motifs in colours as pictured, or in a random arrangement.

D

E

F

G

H

I

Edging

Join yarn B to any corner of the blanket with a ss.

Rnd 1: 3ch, (2tr, 3ch, 3tr) in same sp, * 1ch, [(3tr, 1ch) in next ch-sp or join sp] to next corner sp, ** (3tr, 3ch, 3tr) in next corner sp; rep from * around, ending last rep at **. Join rnd with ss to top of first ch.

Change to yarn C.

Rnd 2: 3ch, (2tr, 3ch, 3tr) in same sp, * 1ch, [(3tr, 1ch) in next ch-sp] to next corner sp, ** (3tr, 3ch, 3tr) in next corner sp; rep from * around, ending last rep at **.

Join rnd with ss to top of first ch.

Change to yarn A and rep Rnd 2.

Change to yarn D and rep Rnd 2.

Change to yarn B and rep Rnd 2.

Fasten off.

FINISHING

Weave in any remaining ends and block lightly to shape.

PATTERN CHART

O chain stitch (ch)

T treble crochet (tr)

• slip stitch (ss)

gadget
COSIES

A gadget case worked in crochet needn't be twee.
These easy-to-hook, bold, graphic cosies are simple,
streamlined and modern.

MATERIALS

You will need a chunky-weight yarn in three colours if you are making both cosies.

Here we have used DMC™ Natura XL, 100% cotton, 100 g/75 m per ball.

    Yarn A: 32 'Natural' x 1 ball
    Yarn B (phone): 07 'Aqua' x 1 ball
    Yarn B (tablet): 42 'Candy' x 1 ball
    Yarn C: 82 'Lime' x 1 ball
6 mm hook
Yarn needle
Sewing needle and matching thread
Button to fasten

YARN ALTERNATIVES

When substituting yarn, you can use the yarn lengths given above as a guide, but the lengths required will vary from one brand of yarn to another. Any chunky weight yarn will substitute here. The tablet and phone cover use 150 g of yarn altogether if a single coloured cosy is desired.

STITCH TECHNIQUES

Chain (ch)
Double crochet (dc)
Working in the round in spirals
Using a stitch marker (m)

GENERAL TIPS

❖ *The button loop makes the gadget cosy easy to open quickly to answer a call or view an email.*

TENSION

Work 11.5dc and 14 rows to measure 10 x 10 cm using a 6 mm hook or the size needed to obtain the correct tension.

FINISHED MEASUREMENTS

Cosies are adaptable to different sized gadgets, but samples shown here are sized as follows:
Tablet Cosy (unstretched): 18 x 25 cm.
Phone Cosy (unstretched): 7 x 13 cm.

PATTERN NOTES

❖ *Cosies are worked in the round in spirals. Do not join the round unless stated otherwise. Place a marker in first stitch of each round and move up each round to mark the beginning of the round.*

❖ *To adapt the pattern to any size of cosy, make the starting chain the same length as the bottom edge of the cosy, then add one chain and follow the main pattern.*

❖ *When making the cosy, ensure that it is slightly smaller or the same size as the gadget for which it is intended, to allow for a snug fit, so that the cosy does not fall off the gadget.*

❖ *Phone cosy instructions are placed outside brackets, tablet cosy instructions are placed inside brackets.*

A

B

PATTERN

With 6 mm hook and yarn A (B), make 8 (20)ch.

Rnd 1: 3dc in second chain from hook, 1dc in each ch to last ch, 3dc in last ch, rotate work 180 degrees so that bottom of the chain can be worked into *(A)*.
1dc in bottom loop of each ch to end *(B)*.
Do not join rnd –16 (40)dc.

Rnd 2: 1dc in first dc, pm *(C)* 1dc in each stitch around – 16 (40)dc.

Rep last Rnd 3 (8) times more. On last rnd, join rnd with ss and fasten off yarn.
Change to yarn B (A).

Rnds 6 (11)–15 (33): As Rnd 2.
On last rnd, join rnd with ss and fasten off yarn.
Join yarn C to central stitch at one side seam.

Rnd 16 (34): 1dc in central side seam stitch, dc to centre of cosy edge, on samples shown it will be 4 (10)dc, 11 (15)ch, ss to bottom of ch, 1dc in each dc to end of rnd, join rnd with ss.
Fasten off yarn and weave in all ends.

FINISHING

Sew the button to the corresponding place on the opposite side of the cosy to the button loop *(D)*.
Insert gadget and fasten button.

C

D

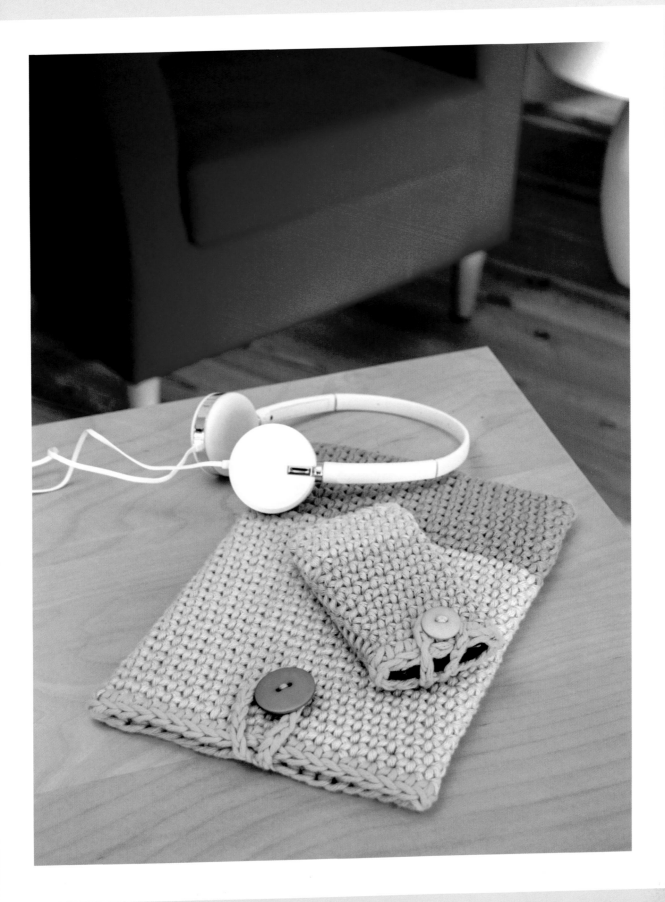

Covered
BANGLES

This project allows you to transform an inexpensive plain plastic bangle into something that becomes a personal style statement.

MATERIALS

You can use any DK weight yarn in any colour.
Here we have used Rico™ Design Essentials Merino
DK, 100% Merino wool, 50 g/120 m.

- Yarn A: 024 'Grey' x 1 ball
- Yarn B: 007 'Orchid' x 1 ball
- Yarn C: 001 'Rose' x 1 ball
- Yarn D: 098 'Silver Grey' x 1 ball

4 mm hook

Yarn needle

Selection of plastic bangles, approximately 8 cm in
diameter and assorted widths.

TENSION

Exact tension is not essential for this pattern, simply
ensure you crochet tightly to create a fabric which
doesn't allow the bangle to show through. A smaller
hook may be needed.

FINISHED MEASUREMENTS

Each bangle is approximately 8 cm in diameter.
Large bangle is approximately 4 cm deep.
Medium bangles are approximately 1 cm deep.
Small bangles are approximately 0.5 cm deep.

YARN ALTERNATIVES

You can use any DK weight yarn to cover bangles.
Very small amounts of each shade are required, so
scraps from stash yarn may be used.

STITCH TECHNIQUES

Chain (ch)
Double crochet (dc)
Half treble crochet (htr)
Clusters (cl)
Working straight in rows
Striping
(See also Special Stitches)

GENERAL TIPS

❖ A covered bangle is a great way to try out new
stitches. Simply work a strip of the stitch that needs
practice, making it large enough to fit the desired
bangle, then sew it around the bracelet.

❖ Each of the bangle patterns shown here can be
adapted to fit different sized bracelets. See pattern
notes for more information.

A

B

C

SPECIAL STITCHES

2 htr Cluster (cl): ** Yoh, Insert hook in next stitch, yoh and draw loop through, (3 loops on hook); (A) rep from * once more, (5 loops on hook), (B), yoh, draw through all 5 loops. (C) Cluster complete.*

PATTERN NOTES

❖ *For Small Bangles, double crochet is worked around the bracelet, as if it is a ring for working in the round. This technique can be worked for any thin bangle.*

❖ *For Medium and Large Bangles, pieces are worked straight until they reach the desired length; then are sewn into place around the bangle.*

❖ *For the Large Bangle, the width of the final piece will fit around the circumference of the bangle, and then be worked upwards to fit around the depth of the bangle.*

❖ *The Large Bangle pattern can be adjusted to fit a thinner or wider bracelet. Simply work more or fewer rows until the strip fits up and around the bracelet.*

❖ *For the Medium Bangle, the width of the final piece will fit around the depth of the bangle, and it can then be worked in rows until it is long enough to fit around the circumference of the bangle.*

❖ *The Medium Bangle pattern can be adjusted to fit a thinner or wider bracelet – simply ensure the starting chain can fit around the width of the bangle, then continue the pattern as normal until the length is the same as the entire circumference of bracelet.*

PATTERN

Large Bangle

With 4 mm hook and Yarn A make 50ch.

Row 1: 1htr in third ch from hook and each ch to end of row, turn – 48htr.

Row 2: 2ch (counts as 1htr), 1htr in each htr to end, turn – 48htr.

Rows 3–6: As row 2.

Row 7: 2ch (counts as 1htr), (1cl [see Special Stitches], 1ch) across next 2 htr] to last st, 1htr in t-ch, turn – 23cl, plus 2htr.

Row 8: 2ch (counts as 1htr), [(1cl, 1ch) across next cl and 1ch] to end, 1htr in t-ch, turn (23cl, plus 2 htr).

Rows 9–12: As row 8.
Fasten off.

Medium Bangle
With 4 mm hook and Yarn B make 11 ch.
Row 1: 1 dc in second ch from hook and each ch to end, turn – 10 dc.
Row 2: 1 ch (does not count as a stitch), 1 dc in each st to end, turn – 10 dc.
Rep Row 2 until strip is long enough to go all round the circumference of the bangle, striping at irregular intervals if required.
Fasten off.

Small Bangle
With 4 mm hook and any shade, attach yarn around bangle with a ss, then insert hook into bangle from front to back, yoh, draw a loop through to front, (2 loops on hook), yoh and draw through both loops, dc around bangle to complete. Continue in this way, making dc around the bangle until it is covered with no gaps. Join rnd with ss to first st.
Fasten off yarn and weave in ends.

FINISHING
For the Medium and Large bangles, wrap crochet pieces around the bangles and sew up the seams with matching yarn using mattress stitch.

Chunky
BASKET TRIO

Baskets are a very simple but practical project. The yarn used is super bulky, so they also work up incredibly fast - you can make one in an evening!

MATERIALS

You will need a superbulky yarn in three colours.
Here we have used Wool and the Gang™ Jersey Be
Good Recycled T-Shirt Yarn, 98% cotton,
2% elastane, 500 g/99.5 m per spool.

> *Yarn A: 'Shiitake Mushroom' x 1 spool*
> *Yarn B: 'Peach Sorbet' x 1 spool*
> *Yarn C: 'Golden Compass' x 1 spool*

9 mm hook
Yarn needle
Stitch marker

YARN ALTERNATIVES

Any superbulky yarn will work here. When substituting yarn, the required lengths will vary from one brand of yarn to another. A yarn can even be made from old T-shirts. Simply cut up an unused tee in a spiral, making a long strip approximately 2 cm wide.

STITCH TECHNIQUES

Chain (ch)
Double crochet (dc)
Back loop only (blo)
Working in rounds (rnds)

GENERAL TIPS

❖ *These chunky baskets can be used to store all sorts of things. They look modern and stylish in the bathroom holding toiletries and cotton wool balls but can be useful in a craft room when used to store yarn, projects and notions or to keep toys tidy in a child's room.*
❖ *The pattern can be easily adapted to make differently sized baskets.*

TENSION

Exact tension is not essential here, but ensure the work is tightly crocheted to make for a stable basket.

FINISHED MEASUREMENTS

Baskets measure approximately 20 (25, 30) cm diameter.

SPECIAL STITCHES

Double crochet in back loop only (dcblo): *Work a dc in back loop only of next st.*
Increase (inc): *2dc in next st.*

PATTERN NOTES

❖ *The bottom of the basket is worked in a flat circle, then a rim is created by working one row in the back loop only, to turn the corner for the sides. Then the sides are worked straight up in spirals, without shaping, until the desired height. Handles are added at the top.*
❖ *Baskets are worked in spirals. Do not join each round or use turning chains unless indicated. Instead, place a marker at the start of the round, moving it upwards each round to denote the beginning of rounds.*

PATTERN

Large basket

With Yarn A and 9 mm hook, make 2ch.

Rnd 1: 6dc in first ch, do not join, pm for working in spirals.

Rnd 2: 2dc in each dc around, do not join rnd – 12dc.

Rnd 3: [Inc (see Special Stitches), 1dc] around – 18dc.

Rnd 4: [Inc, 2dc] around – 24dc.

Rnd 5: [Inc, 3dc] around – 30dc.

Rnd 6: [Inc, 4dc] around – 36dc.

Rnd 7: [Inc, 5dc] around – 42dc.

Rnd 8: [Inc, 6dc] around – 48dc.

Rnd 9: [Inc, 7dc] around, join rnd with ss – 54dc.

Rnd 10: 1ch, 1dcblo (see Special Stitches) in each dc around, join rnd with ss – 54dcblo.

Rnd 11: 1ch, 1dc in each st around, do not join, pm for working in spirals – 54dc.

Rnds 12-15: 1dc in each dc around.

Change to yarn B and work two further rnds as before.

Rnd 18: 10dc, 8ch, miss 7dc, *(A)* 20dc, 8ch, miss 7dc, 1dc in each dc to end of rnd – 40dc and 2 8ch-sps.

Rnd 19: *1dc in each dc to next ch-sp, 10dc in ch-sp *(B)*; rep from * twice, 1dc in each dc to end of rnd, join rnd with ss – 60dc.

Fasten off yarn.

Medium Basket

With Yarn C and 9 mm hook, make 2ch and work as for Large Basket to end of Rnd 6.

Rnd 7: 1ch, 1dcblo in each dc around, join rnd with ss – 36dcblo.

Rnd 8: 1ch, 1dc in each st around, do not join, pm for working in spirals – 36dc.

Rnds 9-15: 1dc in each dc around.

Change to Yarn A.

Rnd 16: 1dc in each dc around.

Rnd 17: 6dc, 8ch, miss 7dc, *(A)* 10dc, 8ch, miss 7dc, 1dc in each dc to end of rnd – 22dc and 2 7ch-sps.

Change to Yarn A.

Rnd 18: *1dc in each dc to next ch-sp, 10dc in ch-sp *(B)*; rep from * twice, 1dc in each dc to end of rnd, join rnd with ss – 42dc.

Fasten off yarn.

Small Basket

With Yarn B and 9 mm hook, make 2ch and work as for Large Basket to end of Rnd 5.

Rnd 6: 1ch, 1dcblo in each dc around, join rnd with ss – 30dcblo.

Rnd 7: 1ch, 1dc in each st around, do not join, pm for working in spirals – 30dc.

Change to Yarn A.

Rnds 8-14: 1dc in each dc around.

On last round, join rnd with ss and fasten off yarn.

FINISHING

Weave in all ends.

A

B

GROWING IN CONFIDENCE

When you have made some of the very basic projects, try your hand at some patterns that use more decorative stitches such as surface crochet – this is used to create textural stripes in the Decorative Coasters. Or create the striking chevrons for the Essential Versatile Wrap – the perfect example of an impressive accessory that uses a stitch that is really very simple to achieve.

Tiny COIN PURSE

Coin purses are tiny and enormously useful. Their small size, and the cuteness that accompanies it, makes them both handy and desirable. This surprisingly easy project is so quick to hook, you will soon be making coin purses as gifts for all your friends.

MATERIALS

You will need DK weight yarn in three colours.
Here we have used Sirdar™ Cotton DK, 100% cotton,
100 g/212 m per ball.

   Yarn A: 507 'Sundance' x 1 ball

   Yarn B: 520 'Grey Dawn' x 1 ball

   Yarn C: 502 'Vanilla' x 1 ball

4 mm hook

Stitch marker

Yarn needle

Attachable metal purse clasp 6 cm

YARN ALTERNATIVES

When substituting yarn, the required lengths will vary from one brand of yarn to another. Any DK weight yarn will work here. Scraps from stash yarn will work well as very small amounts of each shade are required.

STITCH TECHNIQUES

Chain (ch)
Double crochet (dc)
Working in the round in spirals
Increasing (inc)
Adjustable ring
Placing stitch markers (m)
Striping
(See also Special Stitches)

GENERAL TIPS

❖ *Made simply with a long spiral of double crochet in the round, it is easily adaptable by varying the colours and stripes, or working more or fewer rounds.*

TENSION

Exact tension is not essential for this pattern. Simply ensure you crochet tightly to create a stiff fabric with few gaps as this will help to hold the shape when full of coins.

FINISHED MEASUREMENTS

Purse measures 8 cm across.

SPECIAL STITCHES

Increase (inc): *Work 2dc into next stitch.*

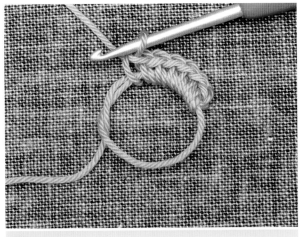

A

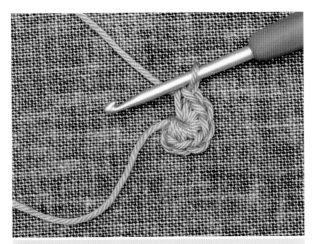

B

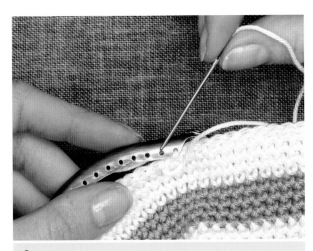

C

PATTERN NOTES

❖ *The purse is worked in the round, in a spiral. Do not join each round or use turning chains. Instead place a marker at the start of the round, moving it upwards each round to denote the beginning of rounds.*
❖ *Work the purse plain or add stripes as shown.*

PATTERN

With 4 mm hook and Yarn A work an adjustable ring – make a loop in your yarn, at least 15 cm from tail end. Insert hook through loop from front to back.
Draw yarn though to front of loop and work 1ch around the loop and the tail end of yarn held double.
Work all following stitches into the ring over the two strands of yarn in the loop.

Rnd 1: 6dc in ring, *(A)* pull up to tighten centre, *(B)* do not join, pm for working in spirals.
Rnd 2: 2dc in each dc around, do not join rnd – 12 dc.
Rnd 3: [Inc (see Special Stitches), 1dc] around – 18 dc.
Rnd 4: [Inc, 2dc] around – 24 dc.
Rnd 5: [Inc, 3dc] around – 30 dc.
Rnd 6: [Inc, 4dc] around – 36 dc.
Change to Yarn B.
Rnds 7–9: 1dc in each dc around.
Change to Yarn C.
Rnds 10–20: 1dc in each dc around.
On last rnd, join with ss and fasten off yarn.
Weave in all ends.

FINISHING

With yarn C and yarn needle, sew the top edge of purse to the open purse frame *(C)*.

TIP

When sewing on the purse frame, flatten the purse opening and mark the two 'corners' made, which will ensure that the edge is split equally in half. This will make it easy to sew the edge into the front and back of the frame evenly.

Patchwork
BLANKET

Practise shaping with these small, portable triangle motifs; then hook them together with a double crochet join to create a striking coverlet.

MATERIALS

You will need a DK to Aran weight yarn in six colours.
Here we have used Debbie Bliss™ Rialto DK,
100% Extra Fine Merino Wool Superwash,
50 g/105 m per ball.

  Yarn A: 09 'Apple' x 2 (5) balls
  Yarn B: 19 'Duck Egg' x 2 (5) balls
  Yarn C: 44 'Aqua' x 2 (5) balls
  Yarn D: 66 'Vintage Pink' x 2 (5) balls
  Yarn E: 69 'Citrus' x 2 (5) balls
  Yarn F: 04 'Grey' x 4 balls
5 mm hook
Yarn needle

YARN ALTERNATIVES

When substituting yarn, the required lengths will vary
from one brand of yarn to another. Any DK to Aran
weight yarn will substitute here, although experimenting
with yarn weights and hook sizes will simply cause the
blanket to come out larger or smaller.

STITCH TECHNIQUES

Chain (ch)
Double crochet (dc)
Double crochet through back loop only (dcblo)
Working in rows
Double crochet join
Double crochet edge
(See also Special Abbreviations)

SPECIAL ABBREVIATIONS

dcblo = Double crochet working through back loop of
the stitch only

GENERAL TIPS

❖ A patchwork-style blanket made from motifs is a
great project for beginners. Duplicating some very
small, simple motifs a number of times to create a
large blanket means that the techniques used will be
mastered very quickly through repetition.

❖ The bold geometric pattern created by the triangles
used here creates a different design to the regular
square patchwork pattern. The triangle shapes add lots
of visual interest with diagonal lines and offers the
chance to play with colour contrasts when up to six
motifs meet in one place.

❖ The single bed size is a labour of love, using over 200
motifs! However, it is a great ongoing project to have
handy when you have some time free. The pattern that
follows can be used to make a lap or baby blanket using
99 motifs, or a blanket for a single bed using 270 motifs.
The single blanket size is always given in brackets. You
could work a different number of motifs for a different
size, or far fewer motifs to make a small cushion.

TENSION

One triangle motif measures approx 11 cm along each
side using a 5 mm hook or the size needed to achieve
the correct tension.

FINISHED MEASUREMENTS

Blanket measures approx 72 (95) x 90 (180) cm.

PATTERN NOTES

❖ *This blanket uses small motifs. You can make it larger or smaller by adding or subtracting motifs. The joining and edging is still worked in the same way.*

❖ *Play with the colours as you wish – this blanket uses motifs with an edging and join in Yarn F to add contrast.*

❖ *1ch does not count as a stitch.*

PATTERN

Triangle motif

Make 99 (270) motifs.

With 5 mm hook and any desired shade apart from yarn F, make 2ch

Row 1: 3dc in secondnd ch from hook, turn – 3dc.

Row 2: 1ch, 1dc in each st to end, turn.

Row 3: 1ch, 2dc in first st, 1dc in each st to last st, 2dc in last st, turn – 5dc.

Row 4: 1ch, 1dc in each st to end, turn.

Rep last two rows until there are 15dc, ending with Row 3.

Edging

1ch, (1dc, 1ch, 1dc) in first st, 1dc in each st to last st, (1dc, 1ch, 1dc) in last st, do not turn, but rotate work and continue along next side of triangle as follows, work 13dc evenly along side of triangle, (1dc, 1ch, 1dc) in bottom of triangle, rotate again and work 13dc up remaining side of triangle, join rnd with ss to first st – 45dc, 3ch.

FINISHING

Weave in any ends and block each triangle lightly to shape.

JOINING

Join 11 (15) triangles into a strip as per joining diagram. To join each triangle, use a double crochet join as follows.

Hold two triangles together with Wrong Side Facing (WSF).

Join Yarn F with a ss to the adjoining points of two triangles, under the 1ch-sp of each triangle together *(A)*. 1ch, then work a dc into the 1ch-sp of each triangle held together. Insert hook under adjoining back loops only of next stitch along of both triangles, held together, then work a **dcblo** (see Special Abbreviations) of each pair of adjoining stitches along to join the side of the triangles *(B)*.

At the next 1ch-sp, work a dc in both 1ch-sps held together at once *(C)*.

A

B

Now take the next triangle, and hold it against just the second triangle, inserting hook back into the 1 ch-sp of the second triangle, and then the adjoining 1 ch-sp of the next triangle at once, working a dc into the space *(D)*.

Insert the hook under the adjoining back loops only of the next stitch along of both triangles, held together, then work a **dcblo** of each pair of adjoining stitches along to join the side of the triangles.

At the next 1 ch-sp, work a dc in both 1 ch-sps held together at once.

Continue in this way, working a dcblo join through each regular stitch of adjoining triangles, and 1 dc join into each 1 ch-sp until 11 (15) triangles are joined in a strip as per joining diagram.

Fasten off yarn.

Now make 9 (18) strips altogether in the same way. Once all the strips are made, join them to each other in rows with yarn F, as shown in the joining diagram. The top and bottom edges are straight and the sides are zig zags. For each join, work a **dcblo** join through every regular stitch and a 1 dc join in each 1 ch-sp.

EDGING

Once all strips are joined, rejoin yarn F to any corner of the blanket with a ss and work one rnd of dc evenly around entire blanket.

Fasten off.

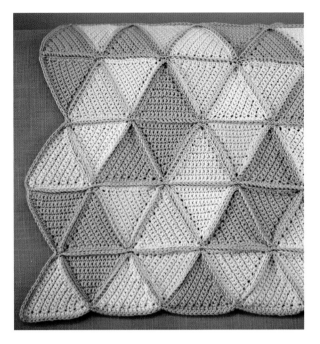

PATCHWORK JOINING CHART

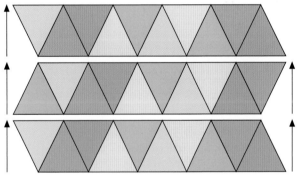

C

D

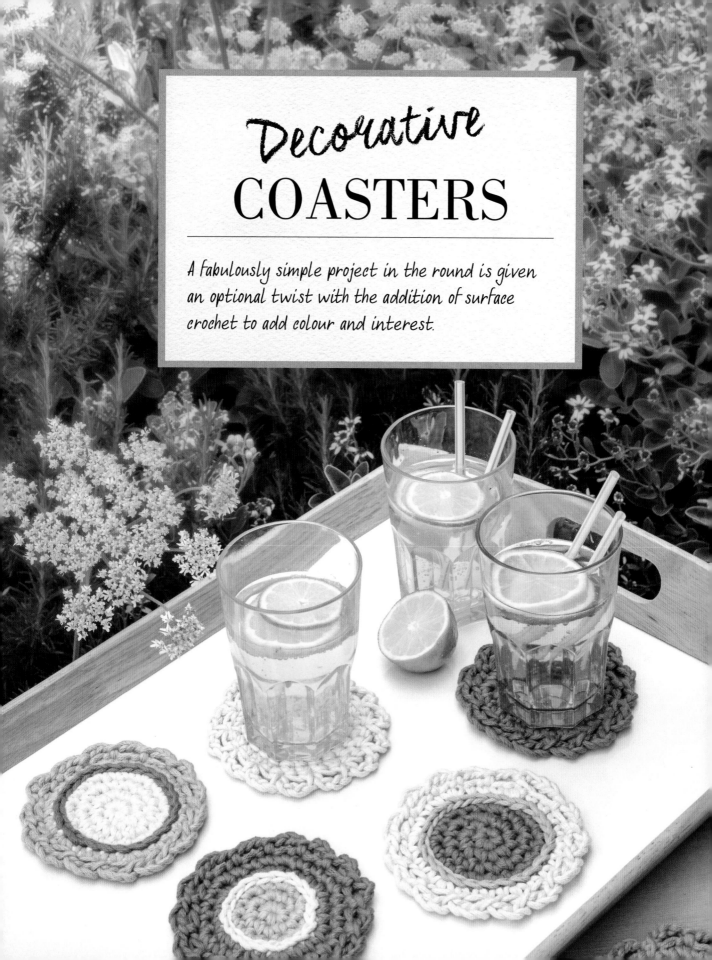

Decorative
COASTERS

A fabulously simple project in the round is given an optional twist with the addition of surface crochet to add colour and interest.

MATERIALS

You will need chunky yarn in three colours.
Here we used DMC™ Natura XL, 100% Cotton,
50 g/75 m per ball.

    Yarn A: 73 (pale blue) x 1 ball
    Yarn B: 07 (teal) x 1 ball
    Yarn C: 71 (dark green) x 1 ball
5.5 mm and 6 mm hooks
Stitch marker
Yarn needle
Pins
Steam iron (optional)

YARN ALTERNATIVES

Any chunky yarn will work here. You can play with the
yarn weight, as changing the weight of the yarn will
simply affect the size of the final coasters. However,
try to choose a mid-weight to chunky yarn and work
with a tight tension so that the coasters are slightly
stiff and robust enough for their purpose.
Each coaster uses approx 15 g of yarn.

STITCH TECHNIQUES

Chain (ch)
Double crochet (dc)
Working in the round in spirals
Adjustable ring
Placing stitch markers (m)
Striping
Surface crochet
Increasing (inc)
(See also Special Abbreviations)

GENERAL TIPS

These simple coasters are worked in a chunky yarn
to make them a perfect way of protecting delicate
surfaces from the heat of hot drinks as well as from
drips and spills.

TENSION

Exact tension is not essential for this pattern.

FINISHED MEASUREMENTS

Coasters measure approx 12 cm in diameter.

PATTERN NOTES

❖ *The coasters are worked in the round, in a spiral.*
Do not join each round or use turning chains; instead
place a marker at the start of the round, moving it
upwards each round to denote rounds.
❖ *Work the coasters plain, as written, or add stripes*
as shown, by changing colour after the third or fourth
round of coaster.
❖ *Surface crochet stripes are optional – follow the steps*
on the following page to create these if desired.

SPECIAL ABBREVIATIONS

Inc: *Increase one stitch by working two stitches into the*
next stitch (in this pattern work 2dc into the next dc).

A

B

C

PATTERN

With 6 mm hook and any desired shade make an adjustable ring.

Rnd 1: 6dc in ring, pull up to tighten centre, do not join, pm for working in spirals.

Rnd 2: 2dc in each dc around, do not join rnd – 12dc.

Rnd 3: [Inc (see Special Abbreviations), 1dc] around – 18dc.

Rnd 4: [Inc, 2dc] around – 24dc.

Rnd 5: [Inc, 3dc] around – 30dc.

Rnd 6: 3ch, *miss next dc, 1dc in next dc, 3ch; rep from * around, join rnd with ss.

FINISHING

Optional

With 5.5 mm hook, surface crochet a chain neatly around the stripe row of each striped coaster with the unused colour from that coaster.

Holding the yarn at the back of the work, insert hook from front to back through fabric at desired starting point of chain *(A)*.

Draw a loop of yarn through to the front of the fabric for first chain *(B)*.

Insert hook through the front of the fabric at desired interval from first insertion point, grab yarn *(C)* and draw a loop through fabric and chain already on hook to secure it *(D)*.

Continue as per *(D)* for entire surface chain, trying to keep chains all the same size by inserting hook at regular intervals. For this pattern, try inserting hook through every stitch of the row you are following.

All coasters

Weave in any remaining ends, pin out petals and block to shape.

Block the coasters thoroughly by dampening slightly, then pinning each of the petals out to the desired shape, making them more prominent *(E)*. Add steam from an iron if desired. Leave to cool and dry before removing the pins.

D

E

Mug
COSIES

A beautiful hand-made mug cosy warms hands in winter when drinking hot drinks, while also making the cup look effortlessly chic.

MATERIALS

You will need Aran weight yarn in three colours.
Here we have used Rico Design™ Creative Cotton
Aran, 100% cotton, 50 g/85 m per ball.

 Yarn A: 61 'Powder' x 1 ball

 Yarn B: 52 'Pearl Grey' x 1 ball

 Yarn C: 60 'Nature' x 1 ball

4.5 mm hook

Yarn needle

One 2 cm button for each cosy

YARN ALTERNATIVES

When substituting yarn, the required lengths will vary
from one brand of yarn to another. Any Aran weight yarn
will work here. Working with small amounts of yarn in
colourful stripes is a great way to use up
stash yarns.

STITCH TECHNIQUES

Chain (ch)

Double crochet (dc)

Treble crochet (tr)

Working straight in rows

Striping

(See also Special Stitches)

GENERAL TIPS

❖ The stitch used in these mug cosies is both modern
and striking. It appears to be complicated to achieve,
especially when worked in stripes, but it is quite simple
to master with a little practice.

❖ A strong geometric pattern is created by the stitches
leaning in different directions, but the stitch is relatively
simple to work.

❖ A project like this is a great one to try out new
stitches as it is small, with no shaping, so it is perfect
for beginners.

TENSION

Exact tension is not essential for this pattern.

FINISHED MEASUREMENTS

Cosy measures 9 x 22 cm.

SPECIAL STITCHES

Double crochet 3 together (dc3tog): Draw up a loop
in each of next 3 stitches, 4 loops on hook, yoh and
draw through all loops on hook. 2 stitches decreased.

PATTERN NOTES

❖ For the striped cosy, work first row in Yarn A,
second row in Yarn B and then alternate A and B
each row. Work edging in Yarn A.

TIP

Try making these cosies with every row a different
colour to create a vibrant, textural pattern that is
sure to brighten up even the plainest of mugs.

PATTERN

With 4.5 mm hook and any yarn, make 49ch.

Row 1 (RS): 2tr in fourth ch from hook, miss 2 ch, 1dc in next ch, * 2ch, 1tr in each of next 3 ch, miss 2ch, 1dc in next ch; rep from * to end, turn – 8 patt reps.

Row 2: 3ch (counts as 1tr), 2tr in same st, *(A)* miss 2 tr, 1dc in next tr, *(B)* * 2ch, 3tr in 2ch-sp, *(C)* miss 2 tr, 1dc in next tr; rep from * to end, turn.

Rows 3–6: As row 2.

Row 7: 3ch (counts as 1tr), 2tr in same st, miss 2 tr, 1dc in next tr, *2ch, 3tr in 2ch-sp, miss 2 tr, 1dc in next tr; rep from * to end, 1ch, ss to top of first stitch of row to join into a round.

Fasten off.

Rotate work 180 degrees, rejoin yarn to bottom right corner with ss and RSF and work along bottom edge as follows:

Edging

Working into bottom loop of base ch, 1dc in same st, 1dc in next ch, 3dc in next ch, 1dc, * dc3tog (see Special Stitches) *(D)*, 1dc, 3dc in next ch, 1dc; rep from * to end, 8ch, ss to bottom of chain.

Fasten off.

Weave in all ends.

FINISHING

Block lightly to shape.

Sew button to cosy on the end of the row opposite the button loop.

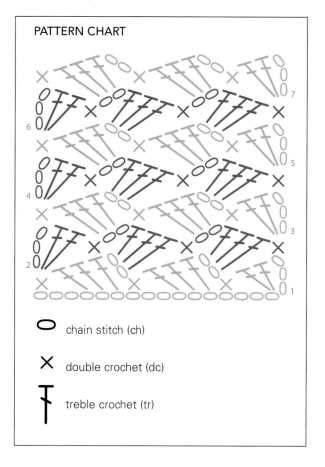

PATTERN CHART

⭕	chain stitch (ch)
✕	double crochet (dc)
⊤	treble crochet (tr)

A

B

C

D

Striped
PENCIL CASE

This striking stripy pencil case is easy to make in yarn of contrasting colours. The fun shape is made in two pieces and the chunky zip will keep everything secure – offering a neat way to store all those loose pencils and pens.

MATERIALS

You will need DK weight yarn in two colours. Here we used Stylecraft™ Classique Cotton DK, 100% cotton, 100 g/184 m per ball.

Yarn A: 3674 'Shrimp' x 1 ball

Yarn B: 3660 'White' x 1 ball

4 mm hook

Stitch marker

Yarn needle

Sewing needle and matching thread

Zip at least 20 cm long

2 circles of card 6 cm in diameter (optional)

YARN ALTERNATIVES

When substituting yarn, the required lengths will vary from one brand of yarn to another. Any Aran weight yarn will substitute here.

STITCH TECHNIQUES

Chain (ch)

Double crochet (dc)

Working in the round in spirals

Working into back loop only

Adjustable ring

Placing stitch markers (m)

Striping

Jogless stripes

(See also Special Stitches)

TENSION

18dc and 20 rows to 10 x 10 cm using a 4 mm hook or the size required to obtain the correct tension.

FINISHED MEASUREMENTS

Pencil Case measures 18 cm long, 6 cm in diameter and 20 cm in circumference.

PATTERN NOTES

❖ *The pencil case is worked in the round in a spiral, except where indicated. Do not join or use turning chains, unless otherwise indicated. Instead, place a marker at the start of the round, moving it upwards each round to denote the beginning of rounds.*

❖ *As the stitches are worked in a spiral pattern around the case, when you change colours you will create a 'jog' in the striping, as the yarn changes from one stitch to the next. You can avoid this by using a 'jogless stripes' technique. Here, you need to join the last round of a stripe with a duplicate stitch, explained overleaf. This will avoid the unsightly 'jog' in your colours.*

❖ *1ch at the beginning of round does not count as a stitch.*

❖ *The pencil case ends are strengthened with card to keep their shape. Inserting the card between the lining and the crocheted ends is optional.*

A

B

C

SPECIAL STITCHES

Increase (inc): *2dc in next stitch.*

Duplicate stitch: *At the end of the row, do not join the round with a slip stitch, but instead draw up the loop on the hook to make it slightly bigger, cut the yarn, leaving the tail end at least 15 cm long (A) and pull the end up through the stitch (B).*

Insert the hook from the back to the front into first stitch of the round, where joining slip stitch is usually worked, yarn over hook (C). Draw a loop through the stitch to the back of the work. Now insert the hook under the back loop only of the last stitch, from the back to the middle of the stitch, (D) yarn over hook.

Draw the end of yarn through the last stitch and pull to create a 'stitch' the same size as all other loops on the row, then weave in the end neatly to secure (E).

PATTERN

Lining (make two)

With 4 mm hook and Yarn A make an adjustable ring.

Rnd 1: 6dc in ring, pull up to tighten centre, do not join, pm for working in spirals.

Rnd 2: 2dc in each dc around, do not join rnd – 12dc.

Rnd 3: [Inc (see Special Stitches), 1dc] around – 18dc.

Rnd 4: [Inc, 2dc] around – 24dc.

Rnd 5: [Inc, 3dc] around – 30dc.

Fasten off yarn.

Pencil Case Bottom

With 4 mm hook and Yarn A make an adjustable ring.

Rnd 1: 6dc in ring, pull up to tighten centre, join rnd with duplicate st (see Special Stitches).

Join in Yarn B with ss in any stitch around.

Rnd 2: 1ch, 2dc in each dc around, do not join rnd, pm for work in spirals – 12dc.

Rnd 3: [Inc, 1dc] around – 18dc.

Rnd 4: [Inc, 2dc] around, join rnd with duplicate st – 24dc.

Join Yarn C with ss in any stitch around.

Rnd 5: 1ch, [inc, 3dc] around, join rnd with ss – 30dc.

Sew lining to bottom piece, with WSF, around last round

of stitches, trapping a circle of card inside for extra strength if desired.

Join Yarn A to Rnd 5 of pencil case bottom.

Rnd 6: 1ch, 1dcblo in each st of Rnd 5, join rnd with ss – 30dcblo.

Rnd 7: 1ch, 1dc in each st around, join rnd with duplicate st – 30dc.

Join Yarn B with ss in any stitch around.

Rnd 8: 1ch, 1dc in each st around, do not join rnd, pm.

Rnd 9: 1dc in each st around, join rnd with duplicate st.

Join Yarn A with ss in any stitch around.

Rnd 10: 1ch, 1dc in each st around, do not join rnd, pm.

Rnd 11: 1dc in each st around, join rnd with duplicate st.

Join Yarn B with ss in any stitch around.

Rep rnds 8–11 five times in total – 28 rows.

Fasten off yarn.

Pencil Case Top

Work as for Pencil Case Bottom for 15 rnds.

Fasten off yarn.

Sew in all ends.

FINISHING

Attach the top of the case to the bottom by sewing in the zip with a backstitch in a loop between the two pencil case pieces.

D

E

Chevron
CLUTCH BAG

A bold chevron design is perfect for an elegant clutch bag to complement your evening wear. Add a decorative brooch for the finishing touch.

MATERIALS

*You will need DK weight cotton yarn in four colours.
Here we have used Sirdar™ Cotton DK, 100% cotton,
100 g/212 m per ball.*

Yarn A: 500 'Black' x 1 ball

Yarn B: 501 'Mill White' x 1 ball

Yarn C: 516 'Tranquil' x 1 ball

Yarn D: 507 'Sundance' x 1 ball

Piece of cotton fabric for the lining 30 x 45 cm

3.5 mm hook

Yarn needle

Pins

Sewing needle and matching thread

15 mm press stud

YARN ALTERNATIVES

*When substituting yarn, the required lengths will vary
from one brand of yarn to another. Any DK weight
cotton yarn will substitute here, although experimenting
with yarn weights and hook sizes will simply cause the
bag to come out bigger or smaller.*

*The yarn used here is mercerised, making it strong
and shiny – both properties are great for this project,
the strength means that the fabric will be less likely to
stretch out of shape when carrying heavy items like
keys, and the sheen lends a dressy quality that makes
the bag perfect for evening wear.*

STITCH TECHNIQUES

Chain (ch)

Double crochet (dc)

Half treble crochet (htr)

Treble crochet (tr)

Working straight

Chevrons

Increasing (inc)

Decreasing (dec)

Stripes

(See also Special Stitches)

GENERAL TIPS

❖ *Working a chevron, zig zag or ripple pattern is a
great way to practise shaping, as this crisp, geometric
stitch is achieved by increasing and decreasing stitches
across the row. Always worked at the same point, the
increases create 'peaks' and the decreases create
'troughs'. Keep a close watch on the placement of the
increases and decreases to ensure the stitch is always
worked correctly – decreases should be worked on top
of decreases, and increases on top of increases.*

❖ *It's a good idea to count the stitches regularly as
with all the increasing and decreasing it can be easy
to make a mistake!*

❖ *Here, the chevron is worked using a double crochet
stitch, so the very simple decrease method of missing
stitches is used. Double crochet is a short stitch so gaps
created by missed stitches are not very noticeable.*

❖ *Chevron stitch creates a fabric with a zig zag hem.
This bag requires straight sides, so these are 'filled in'
afterwards, but when working other projects, they can
be left uneven to give an attractive edge.*

❖ *To make the zig zag even sharper, this particular
chevron pattern works some rows into the back loop
of the stitch only.*

TENSION

*Work 22dc and 24 rows to measure 10 x 10 cm in
double crochet using a 3.5 mm hook or the size
needed to obtain the correct tension.*

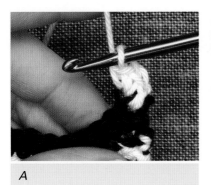

A

B

C

FINISHED MEASUREMENTS

Bag measures 28 cm wide by 22 cm deep.

SPECIAL STITCHES

Back loop only (blo): *Work into the back loop only of next st.*

Double crochet two together (dc2tog): *Draw up a loop through each of next 2 stitches, (3 loops on hook), yoh, draw through all loops on hook.*

Chevron pattern

Pattern Row 1: *1ch, 2dc in blo of first dc, (A) 3dcblo, (B) miss 2 dc, 3dcblo, (C) * 3dc in blo of next st, (D) 3dcblo, miss 2dc, 3dcblo; rep from * to last stitch, 2dc in last st, (E) turn.*

Pattern Row 2: *1ch, 2dc in first dc, 3dc, miss 2 dc, 3dc, * 3dc in next st, 3dc, miss 2dc, 3dc; rep from * to last stitch, 2dc in last st, turn.*

Repeat Rows 1 and 2 for desired length of chevron pattern changing colour as required.

PATTERN NOTES

❖ *The body of the bag is worked in one piece, straight, then the top and bottom edges are filled in, and the flap is worked. Finally, the bag is lined with cotton fabric for added strength and to create an eye-catching interior and then folded and sewn along the two sides to create the bag.*

❖ *1ch at beginning of row does not count as stitch.*

PATTERN

Main bag body

With 4 mm hook and Yarn A, make 74ch.

Row 1 (RS): 2dc in second ch from hook, 3dc, miss next ch, 3dc, * 3dc in next ch, 3dc, miss next ch, 3dc; rep from * to last ch, 2dc in last ch, turn – 82dc.

Row 2: 1ch, 2dc in first dc, 3dc, miss 2 dc, 3dc, * 3dc in next st, 3dc, miss 2dc, 3dc; rep from * to last stitch, 2dc in last st, turn.

Change to yarn B.

Rows 3–24: Rep Pattern Rows 1 & 2 of Chevron pattern

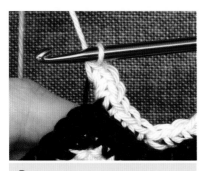

D

E

TIP

Count the stitches in between each increase and decrease – there should be three double crochet in between each peak and trough.

(see Special Stitches), alternating between Yarn A and Yarn B every 2 rows.

Change to Yarn C and work Pattern Rows 1 and 2 of Chevron pattern.

Change to Yarn D and work Pattern Rows 1 and 2 of Chevron pattern.

Rows 29–38: Beg with Yarn A, Rep Pattern Rows 1 & 2 of Chevron pattern, alternating between Yarn A and Yarn B every 2 rows.

Rows 39 & 40: Change to Yarn D and work Pattern Rows 1 and 2 of Chevron pattern.

Rows 41–42: Change to Yarn C and work Pattern Rows 1 and 2 of Chevron pattern.

Rows 43–66: Beg with Yarn B, Rep Pattern Rows 1 & 2 of Chevron pattern, alternating between Yarn B and Yarn A every 2 rows, last 2 rows should be in Yarn A.

Row 67: 1ch, 1dc in first dc, * miss next dc, 1htr, 4tr, 1htr, miss next dc, 1dc; rep from * across row – 64sts. Fasten off.

Rejoin yarn A to bottom of strip with ss and work as Row 67, do not fasten off.

Flap

Row 1: 1ch, 1dc in first st, miss next st, 1dc in each st to last 2 dc, miss next dc, 1dc in last dc, turn – 62dc. Rep last row until 4 sts rem.

Next row: 1ch, (dc2tog [see Special Stitches]) twice.

Next row: 1ch, dc2tog.

Fasten off and weave in all ends.

FINISHING

Block the piece lightly to shape. Hem the fabric piece and sew to the main body of the bag, with Wrong Side Facing (WSF). Leave the flap unlined. Fold the bottom of the main body of the bag up to the bottom of the flap and sew up two side seams. Match up the zig zag stripes for neatness. Fold down the flap and sew the press stud under the flap to fasten.

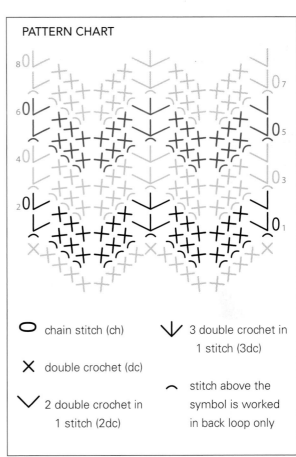

PATTERN CHART

$\bigcirc$ chain stitch (ch)	$\downarrow\!\!\!\vee$ 3 double crochet in 1 stitch (3dc)
$\times$ double crochet (dc)	
$\vee$ 2 double crochet in 1 stitch (2dc)	$\frown$ stitch above the symbol is worked in back loop only

Essential
VERSATILE WRAP

This very desirable wrap can be worn in many different ways. It fits perfectly around the shoulders like a poncho or cape, or may be worn draped casually around the neck like a cowl or infinity scarf.

MATERIALS

You will need super chunky weight wool or wool mix yarn in two colours.

Here we have used Debbie Bliss™ Roma, 70% wool, 30% alpaca, 100 g/80 m per ball.

  Yarn A: 03 'Steel' x 3 balls

  Yarn B: 08 'Citrus' x 1 ball

10 mm hook

Yarn needle

Stitch marker

Pins

YARN ALTERNATIVES

When substituting yarn, the required lengths will vary from one brand of yarn to another. Any super chunky weight wool or wool mix will substitute here, although experimenting with yarn weights and hook sizes will simply cause the wrap to come out bigger or smaller.

STITCH TECHNIQUES

Chain (ch)

Double crochet (dc)

Half treble crochet (htr)

Working in the round in spirals

Using stitch markers (m)

Striping

Tweed stitch

GENERAL TIPS

❖ *The simple shape of this chunky wrap means it can be worn over a coat, or in place of one.*

❖ *The tweed stitch used to create the 'dots' of colour around the hem looks like a complex technique, but it is simply made using only the basic double crochet and chain stitches. Stripes form the colour pops.*

TENSION

Work 8.5 sts and 10 rows in tweed stitch to measure 10 x 10cm using a 10 mm hook or the size needed to obtain the correct tension.

FINISHED MEASUREMENTS

To fit S (M, L).
The wrap measures 40 cm long and 100 (110, 120) cm around the hem.

PATTERN NOTES

❖ *The tweed stitch section is worked in the round in spirals.*
❖ *Do not join each round or use turning chains unless otherwise stated. Instead, place a marker at the start of the round, moving it upwards each round to denote the rounds.*
❖ *There are three sizes given here. Measure around the top of the body, around the fullest part of the chest, including around the arms, to decide on the size to fit. Choose a size slightly bigger than the actual measurement.*

TIP

When you start a new project and you are choosing new yarns, it's a good idea to write down the yarn you are using, listing the manufacturer, the colour and the weight of the yarn. If you decide to change the colours in a pattern, then note what colours you have substituted – this is really useful when you come back to the project later.

A

B

PATTERN

With 10 mm hook and **Yarn A**, make 85 (93, 101)ch and join into a round with a ss, being careful not to twist round.

Rnd 1: 2ch (counts as 1htr), 1htr in each ch around, join rnd with a ss to top of first ch – 85 (93, 101)htr.

Rnd 2: 2ch (counts as 1htr), 1htr in each htr around, join rnd with a ss to top of first ch – 85 (93, 101)htr.

Rnd 3: As rnd 2.

Rnd 4: 2ch (counts as 1dc, 1ch), *(A)* miss next st, * 1dc in next st, 1ch, *(B)* miss next st; rep from * around, do not join rnd.

Change to yarn B.

Rnd 5: 1dc in first 1ch-sp, pm to denote first st of rnd, 1ch, *(C)* *1dc in next 1ch-sp, 1ch; *(D)* rep from * around, do not join rnd.

Change to Yarn A.

Rnds 6-7: [1dc in next 1ch-sp, 1ch] around.

Change to Yarn B.

Rnd 8: As rnds 6–7.

Change to yarn A.

Rnds 9–11: As rnds 6–8.

Change to yarn A.

Rnds 12–27: [1dc in next 1ch-sp, 1ch] around.

Rnd 28: 1dc in each dc and ch around – 85 (93, 101)dc.

Rnd 29: [8 (9, 10)dc, dc2tog] to last 5 sts, 5dc

– 77 (85, 93)dc.

Rnd 30: [7 (8, 9)dc, dc2tog] to last 5 sts, 5dc – 69 (77, 85)dc.

Rnd 31: [6 (7, 8)dc, dc2tog] to last 5 sts, 5dc – 61 (69, 77)dc.

Rnd 32: [5 (6, 7)dc, dc2tog] to last 5 sts, 5dc – 53 (61, 69)dc.

Rnd 33: [4 (5, 6)dc, dc2tog] to last 5 sts, 5dc – 45 (53, 61)dc.

Rnds 34 & 35: 1dc in each dc around.

Fasten off yarn and weave in all ends.

FINISHING

Block lightly to shape.

C

D

HOOKED
ON CROCHET

By now you are sure to be hopelessly addicted to crocheting and the projects here will gently test your newly learned skills, while still being quite simple to create. For example, the pretty V-Stitch Cushion Cover uses a lovely lace stitch and candy stripes, while the Shaped Lace Collar uses a mixture of simple stitches to create a unique and quick-to-make statement accessory.

Stretchy
SHOPPING BAG

A large shopper is a practical accessory for fitting in all those grocery essentials. The subtle geometric lace pattern in this bag is made by simply missing out certain stitches, using a chain space to jump over them.

MATERIALS

You will need DK weight cotton yarn in four colours. Here we have used Debbie Bliss™ Cotton DK, 100% cotton, 50 g/84 m per ball.

- *Yarn A: 61 'Aqua' x 3 balls*
- *Yarn B: 09 'Duck Egg' x 1 ball*
- *Yarn C: 75 'English Mustard' x 1 ball*
- *Yarn D: 20 'Avocado' x 1 ball*

4 mm and 4.5 mm hooks

Yarn needle

Stitch marker

Pins

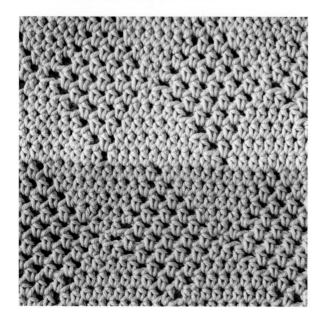

YARN ALTERNATIVES

When substituting yarn, the required lengths will vary from one brand of yarn to another. A DK weight cotton yarn will substitute here, although experimenting with yarn weights and hook sizes will simply cause the bag to come out bigger or smaller.

STITCH TECHNIQUES

Chain (ch)
Double crochet (dc)
Half treble crochet (htr)
Working straight
Working in the round
Increasing (inc)
Decreasing (dec)
Stripes
(See also Special Stitches)

TENSION

Work 16dc and 20 rows straight in double crochet to measure 10 x 10 cm using a 4 mm hook or the size needed to obtain the correct tension.

FINISHED MEASUREMENTS

Bag measures 30 cm in diameter across the bottom, and is approximately 50 cm long.

A

B

C

SPECIAL STITCHES

Double crochet two together (dc2tog): *Draw up a loop through each of next 2 stitches, (3 loops on hook), yoh, draw through all loops on hook.*

Inc: *Work two dc in next stitch.*

PATTERN NOTES

❖ *The body of the bag is worked in the round in one piece. The double crochet section is worked in spirals. The half treble lace section is worked in joined rounds. The yarn is rejoined to top edge of the body and then the handles are worked straight in rows.*

❖ *For rounds worked in spirals, do not join each round or use turning chains; instead place a marker at the start of the round, moving it upwards each round to denote the beginning of rounds.*

PATTERN

Main bag body

With 4mm hook and Yarn A, make 2ch.

Rnd 1: 6dc in second ch from hook, do not join, pm for working in spirals – 6dc.

Rnd 2: 2dc in each dc around, do not join rnd – 12dc.

Rnd 3: [Inc (see Special Stitches), 1dc] around – 18 dc.

Rnd 4: [Inc, 2dc] around – 24 dc.

Rnd 5: [Inc, 3dc] around – 30 dc.

Rnd 6: [Inc, 4dc] around – 36 dc.

Rnd 7: [Inc, 5dc] around – 42 dc.

Continue in this way, for 28 rnds with one stitch more between increases each round, until there are 132 sts. Change to 4.5 mm hook and Yarn B.

Rnd 29: 2ch, (counts as 1htr), 10htr, 1ch, [11htr, 1ch] around, join rnd with ss to first st (132htr and 12 1ch-sps).

Rnd 30: 3ch (counts as 1htr, 1ch), miss next htr, * 9htr, 1ch, miss next htr, 1htr in ch-sp, 1ch, miss next htr; rep from * around, join rnd with ss.

Rnd 31: Ss to next ch-sp, 3ch (counts as 1htr, 1ch), *miss next htr, 7htr, 1ch, miss next htr, [1htr in ch-sp, 1ch] twice; rep from * around, ending last rep with [1htr in ch-sp, 1ch], join rnd with ss.

Rnd 32: Ss to next ch-sp, 3ch (counts as 1htr, 1ch), * miss next htr, 5htr, 1ch, miss next htr, [1htr in ch-sp, 1ch] three times; rep from * around *(A–E)*, ending last rep with [1htr in ch-sp, 1ch] twice, join rnd with ss.

Rnd 33: Ss to next ch-sp, 3ch (counts as 1htr, 1ch), * miss next htr, 3htr, 1ch, miss next htr, [1htr in ch-sp, 1ch] four times; rep from * around, ending last rep with [1htr in ch-sp, 1ch] three times, join rnd with ss.

Rnd 34: Ss to next ch-sp, 3ch (counts as 1htr, 1ch), * miss next htr, 1htr, 1ch, miss next htr, [1htr in ch-sp, 1ch] five times; rep from * around, ending last rep with [1htr in ch-sp, 1ch] four times, join rnd with ss.

Rnd 35: Ss to next ch-sp, 2ch (counts as 1htr), * 1htr, [1htr in ch-sp, 1ch] five times, ** 1htr in ch-sp; rep from * around, ending last rep at ** join rnd with ss.

Rnd 36: 2ch (counts as 1htr), 2htr, *[1htr in ch-sp, 1ch] four times, 1htr in ch-sp, ** 3htr; rep from * around, ending last rep at **, join rnd with ss.

Rnd 37: 2ch (counts as 1htr), 3htr, * [1htr in ch-sp, 1ch] three times, 1htr in ch-sp, 5htr; rep from * around, ending last rep with 1htr in ch-sp, 1htr, join rnd with ss.

Rnd 38: 2ch (counts as 1htr), 4htr, * [1htr in ch-sp, 1ch] twice, 1htr in ch-sp, 7htr; rep from * around, ending last rep with 1htr in ch-sp, 2htr, join rnd with ss.

Rnd 39: 2ch (counts as 1htr), 1htr, pm in this st, 4htr, * 1htr in ch-sp, 1ch, 1htr in ch-sp, 9htr; rep from * around, ending last rep with 1htr in ch-sp, 3htr, join rnd with ss.

Fasten off Yarn B.

Join Yarn B to marked htr with ss.

Rnd 40: 2ch (counts as 1htr), 10htr, 1ch, miss next htr, [11htr, 1ch, miss next htr] around, join rnd with ss – 132htr and 12 1ch-sps.

Rep Rnds 30-39 once more.

Fasten off Yarn C.

Join Yarn D to marked htr with ss.

Next Rnd: As Rnd 40.

Rep Rnds 30–39 once more.

Change to 4 mm hook and rejoin Yarn A to any htr from last rnd.

Next Rnd: 1ch, 1dc in each htr around, missing all the ch-sps, do not join rnd, pm for work in spirals – 132dc.

Work 2 rnds straight in dc.

Next Rnd: [9dc, **dc2tog** (see Special Stitches)] around – 120dc.

Work 1 rnd straight in dc.

Next Rnd: [8dc, dc2tog] around – 108dc.

Work 1 rnd straight in dc.

Next Rnd: [7dc, dc2tog] around – 96dc.

Work 2 rnds straight in dc.

Do not fasten off.

D

E

Handles

Row 1: 20dc, turn, leaving rem sts unworked – 20dc.

Row 2: 1ch, (does not count as st) dc2tog, 16dc, dc2tog, turn – 18dc.

Row 3: 1ch, (does not count as st), 1dc in each dc to end, turn.

Row 4: 1ch, (does not count as st) dc2tog, 14dc, dc2tog, turn – 16dc.

Row 5: 1ch, (does not count as st), 1dc in each dc to end, turn.

Row 6: 1ch, (does not count as st) dc2tog, 12dc, dc2tog, turn – 14dc.

Row 7: 1ch, (does not count as st), 1dc in each dc to end, turn.

Row 8: 1ch, (does not count as st) dc2tog, 10dc, dc2tog, turn – 12dc.

Continue on these 12 sts until handle measures 28 cm/11 inches from Row 1, or desired length. Fasten off yarn.

[Rejoin yarn A to fifth stitch along from beginning of last handle and rep from Row 1] three times.

FINISHING

Block pieces lightly to shape.

Place the two adjoining handle pieces together with Wrong Side Facing (WSF) and join the top edges together with a slip stitch join.
Rep for the remaining two handle pieces.

PATTERN CHART

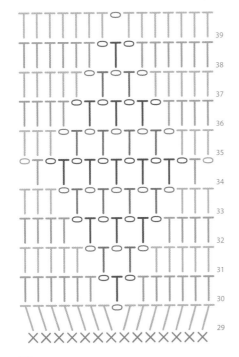

O   chain stitch (ch)

X   double crochet (dc)

T   half treble crochet (htr)

TIP

The tight double crochet stitch should reduce the stretch of the crochet fabric, but a cotton fabric lining can always be inserted to add strength. Try a contrasting colour, which will show through the lace holes.

Fingerless GLOVES

Fingerless gloves are a really practical alternative to traditional gloves in cold weather – the hands are kept snug and warm while still retaining their ability to work a smart phone, to fasten buttons or even to crochet!

MATERIALS

You will need a soft DK weight yarn in any colour. Here we have used Artesano™ DK Alpaca, 100% superfine alpaca, 50 g/100 m per ball.

Shade: SFN41 'Bonbon' x 1 ball

4 mm hook

Yarn needle

Stitch marker

6 x 10 mm diameter buttons

YARN ALTERNATIVES

When substituting yarn, the required lengths will vary from one brand of yarn to another. Any DK weight yarn will substitute here, make sure the yarn is soft and warm to ensure the gloves' comfort and thermal properties. Experimenting with yarn weights and hook sizes will simply cause the gloves to come out bigger or smaller.

STITCH TECHNIQUES

Chain (ch)

Double crochet (dc)

Back loop only (blo)

Working in rows

Working in rounds (rnds)

(See also Special Stitches)

GENERAL TIPS

❖ *Gloves can be a tricky project to master, but when the complicated fingers are removed, they become a breeze!*

TENSION

Work 22dc and 22 rows to measure 10 x 10 cm using a 4 mm hook or the size needed to achieve the correct tension.

FINISHED MEASUREMENTS

S (M, L)

Gloves are approximately 15 cm long and 20 (21, 22) cm around at widest part of the hand.

Gloves should stretch slightly to fit for snug and comfortable wear.

The length can be adapted slightly to fit perfectly (see Pattern Notes).

SPECIAL STITCHES

Buttonloop: *5ch, ss to bottom of chain.*

Double crochet in front loop only (dcflo): *Work a dc in front loop only of next st.*

Double crochet in back loop only (dcblo): *Work a dc in back loop only of next st.*

Increase (inc): *2dcblo in next st – working both stitches into back loop only of next st.*

Double crochet three sts together (dc3tog): *Draw up a loop in each of next 3 sts, (4 loops on hook), yoh and draw through all loops at once to decrease 2 sts.*

PATTERN NOTES

❖ *The glove cuffs are worked straight, in rows.*

❖ *The hand of the glove is worked in the round in spirals. Do not join each round or use turning chains unless indicated; instead place a marker at the start of the round, moving it upwards each round to denote the beginning of rounds.*

❖ *The glove can be adapted in length to fit perfectly. When the thumb gusset shaping is finished, work without shaping where indicated until the length of the glove is at the bottom of the thumb.*

❖ *After finishing the thumb, work the hand to the desired length where indicated. Keep trying on the glove to obtain the perfect fit.*

❖ *1ch at beg of rnd does not count as a stitch.*

PATTERN

LEFT GLOVE

Cuff

With 4 mm hook, make 32 (34, 36)ch.

Row 1 (RS): 1dc in second ch from hook and each ch to end, work **buttonloop** (see Special Stitches), turn – 31 (33, 35)dc plus 5ch buttonloop.

Row 2: 1ch, **1dcflo** (see Special Stitches) in each dc to end, turn – 31 (33, 35)dcflo.

Row 3: 1ch, **1dcblo** (see Special Stitches) in each dc to end, work buttonloop, turn – 31 (33, 35)dcflo plus 5ch buttonloop.

Rows 4 & 5: As rows 2 & 3.

Row 6: 1ch, 1dcflo in each dc to end, turn – 31 (33, 35)dcflo.

Thumb gusset shaping

Rnd 1: 1ch, 1dcblo in each st across, ss to first st to join to work in the round, do not turn.

Rnd 2: 1ch, 14 (15, 16)dcblo, inc (see Special Stitches), 1dcblo, inc, 14 (15:16) dcblo, do not join rnd, but place marker for working in spirals and continue working in spirals from now on for thumb gusset, moving marker up each rnd – 33 (35, 37)dcblo.

Rnd 3: 1dcblo in each st around.

Rnd 4: 14 (15, 16)dcblo, inc, 3dcblo, inc, 14(15, 16)dcblo – 35 (37, 39)dcblo.

Rnd 5: 1dcblo in each st around.

Rnd 6: 14 (15, 16)dcblo, inc, 5dcblo, inc, 14 (15, 16)dcblo – 37 (39, 41)dcblo.

Rnd 7: 1dcblo in each st around.

Rnd 8: 14 (15, 16)dcblo, inc, 7dcblo, inc, 14 (15, 16)dcblo – 39 (41, 43)dcblo.

Rnd 9: 1dcblo in each st around.

Rnd 10: 14 (15, 16)dcblo, inc, 9dcblo, inc, 14 (15, 16)dcblo – 41 (43, 45)dcblo.

Rnd 11: 1dcblo in each st around.

Rnd 12: 14 (15, 16)dcblo, inc, 11dcblo, inc, 14 (15, 16)dcblo – 43 (45, 47)dcblo).

Rnd 13: 1dcblo in each st around.

Rnd 14: 14 (15, 16)dcblo, inc, 13dcblo, inc, 14 (15, 16)dcblo – 45 (47, 49)dcblo.

Work 4 rnds without shaping, or until desired length to bottom of thumb.

Hand

Next Rnd: 16 (17, 18)dcblo, 1ch, miss next 13sts for thumb, 16 (17, 18)dcblo – 32 (34, 36)dcblo plus 1ch.

Next Rnd: 16 (17, 18)dcblo, 1dc in 1ch, 16 (17, 18)dcblo – 33 (35, 37)sts.

Next Rnd: 1dcblo in each st around – 33 (35, 37)dcblo. Rep last Rnd six further times or until hand is desired length to bottom of fingers.

Fasten off.

Thumb

Rejoin yarn to thumb stitches, in the dc to the right of 1ch from hand stitches, **dc3tog** (see Special Stitches) inserting hook in st that yarn was joined to, into bottom loop of 1ch from hand, and into next thumb stitch, work 11dcblo around rem thumb stitches join rnd with ss – 12sts.

Fasten off.

RIGHT GLOVE

Cuff

With 4 mm hook, make 32 (34, 36)ch.

Row 1 (RS): 1dc in second ch from hook and each ch to end, turn – 31 (33, 35)dc.

Row 2: 1ch, 1dcflo in each dc to end, work button loop, turn – 31 (33, 35)dcflo plus 5ch button loop.

Row 3: 1ch, 1dcblo in each dc to end, turn – 31 (33, 35) dcblo.

Rows 4 & 5: As rows 2 & 3.

Row 6: 1ch, 1dcflo in each dc to end, work button loop, turn – 31 (33, 35)dcflo plus 5ch button loop.

Finish as for Left Glove from Thumb Gusset Shaping.

FINISHING

Weave in all ends and sew buttons to cuff at corresponding points to button loops *(A)*.

A

V-Stitch
CUSHION COVER

Assorted cushions in both plain and striped colour ways look very striking and add colour to any interior. Working a V-stitch in stripes creates a stunning effect that looks very complicated, but in fact is relatively simple.

MATERIALS

You will need DK to Aran/worsted weight yarn in four colours.

Here we have used Debbie Bliss™ Mia, 50% cotton, 50% wool, 50 g/100 m per ball.

Yarn A: 17 'Aqua' x 2 balls

Yarn B: 12 'Peach' x 1 ball

Yarn C: 22 'Silver' x 1 ball

Yarn D: 11 'Light Pink' x 1 ball

4.5 mm hook

Yarn needle

Sewing needle and matching thread

Cushion pad 45 x 45 cm

6 buttons approx 2.5 cm diameter

YARN ALTERNATIVES

When substituting yarn, the required lengths will vary from one brand of yarn to another. Experimenting with yarn weights and hook sizes will simply cause the cushion cover to come out bigger or smaller. Any DK to Aran/worsted weight yarn will work well here, check your tension well before beginning. If a single coloured cushion is desired, the total weight of yarn used in the piece is 200 g, or 4 balls.

STITCH TECHNIQUES

Chain (ch)

Double crochet (dc)

Treble crochet (tr)

Working in rows

Striping

Edging

Working into back loop only (blo)

(See also Special Stitches)

GENERAL TIPS

❖ The contrast edging gives the cushion a neat and professional-looking finish with minimal fuss.

❖ Alternatively, the cushion could be made in a single colour, without stripes, but with piping in a contrasting colour, which would look equally as attractive.

TENSION

Work 5 V stitches and 7 rows to measure 10 x 10 cm using a 4.5 mm hook or the size needed to obtain the correct tension.

A

B

C

FINISHED MEASUREMENTS

Finished cushion cover measures 45 x 45 cm. Final cushion pieces will measure approx 40 x 40 cm, but will stretch to fit over cushion pad for a snug, attractive fit.

SPECIAL STITCHES

V stitch (Vst): *(1tr, 1ch, 1tr) all in next st. (A and B) When working into a Vst, work into the 1ch-sp of Vst in row below. (C)*

Dc through back loops only (dcblo): *Insert hook through back loop of each stitch only.*

PATTERN NOTES

❖ *Either the buttoned side or the plain side can be used as the front of the cushion, as desired.*

❖ *Stripe Sequence:*

    Yarn A, Yarn B, Yarn C, Yarn D

❖ *The Right Side of each piece is whichever side is facing when it is edged in Yarn A.*

PATTERN

Plain side

With 4.5 mm hook and Yarn A, make 64ch.

Row 1: 1**Vst** (see Special Stitches) in sixth ch from hook, miss 2 ch, * 1Vst in next ch, miss 2ch; rep from * to last ch, 1tr in last ch, turn – 20 Vst, 2 tr.

Change to yarn B.

Row 2: 3ch (counts as 1tr here and throughout), [1Vst in next Vst] to last st, 1tr in top of t-ch, turn.

Change to Yarn C.

Row 3: As Row 2.

Change to Yarn D.

Row 4: As Row 2.

Continue in pattern, repeating Row 2 in stripe sequence until 28 rows have been worked in total.

Fasten off yarn.

Join yarn A to any stitch around edge.

Edging (RS): 1ch, work evenly in dc all around edge of piece, working 3dc in each corner space, join rnd with ss.

Buttoned side (two pieces)

Bottom

With 4.5 mm hook and Yarn A, make 64ch.
Work as Plain Side for 14 rows.
Change to Yarn A.
Row 15: 1ch (does not count as st), 1dc in each tr
and ch-sp across row, turn – 61dc.
Edging (RS): 1ch, work evenly in dc all around edge
of piece, working 3dc in each corner space, join rnd
with ss.

Top

With 4.5 mm hook and Yarn A, make 62ch.
Row 1: 1dc in second ch from hook and each ch to end
– 61dc.
Row 2: 3ch, miss 2dc, * 1Vst in next dc, miss 2dc;
rep from * to last dc, 1tr in last dc, turn – 20 Vst, 2 tr.
Change to Yarn B.
Row 3: 3ch, [1Vst in next Vst] to last st, 1tr in top of
t-ch, turn.
Change to Yarn C and complete 12 further rows
(14 Vst rows in total) of Vst pattern in stripe sequence
as before.
Fasten off yarn.
Join yarn A to any stitch around edge.
Edging (RS): 1ch, work evenly in dc all around edge
of piece, working 3dc in each corner space, join rnd
with ss.

FINISHING

Pin the bottom piece to the bottom of the plain piece
with WSF, then pin the top piece to the top of the plain
piece with WSF, overlapping the dc rows at the centre.
Now, with Yarn A and a 4.5 mm hook, join the pieces
together with a double crochet join through adjoining
back loops of each stitch only as follows:
Join yarn A to any stitch around the edge with a ss.
Insert hook through adjoining back loops only of next
dc from front piece of fabric and back piece of fabric.

Yoh and draw loop through both stitches to front,
2 lps on hook.
Yoh and draw through both loops to complete
dcblo join.
Continue in this way, working a dcblo join in every
pair of stitches around entire outside edge of cushion.
At the point where the top and bottom pieces overlap,
insert hook through entire stitch of both top and bottom
pieces, but only the back loop of the plain piece.

Fasten off the yarn and weave in all ends. Add six
buttons at regular intervals along top Vst row of the
bottom piece.
Insert a cushion pad and fasten the buttons by inserting
them through the holes at the centre of Vsts.

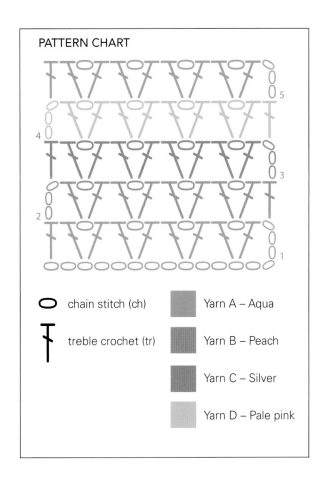

PATTERN CHART

$\bigcirc$	chain stitch (ch)		Yarn A – Aqua
T	treble crochet (tr)		Yarn B – Peach
			Yarn C – Silver
			Yarn D – Pale pink

Shaped LACE COLLAR

This beautiful bold lace collar can be applied around the neckline of a plain T-shirt or worn separately as a modern statement necklace, making it very versatile as well as incredibly pretty.

MATERIALS

You will need a DK weight yarn in any colour. Here we have used Rowan™ Handknit Cotton, 100% cotton, 50 g/85 m per ball.

Shade: 352 'Sea Foam' x 1 ball

4 mm hook

Pins

YARN ALTERNATIVES

When substituting yarn, the required lengths will vary from one brand of yarn to another. Any DK weight yarn will work here, although experimenting with yarn weights and hook sizes will simply cause the collar to come out bigger or smaller. Try a luxury yarn, such as silk, for an extravagant evening wear alternative.

STITCH TECHNIQUES

Chain (ch)
Double crochet (dc)
Treble crochet (tr)
Working in rows
Bobble
(See also Special Stitches)

GENERAL TIPS

❖ *Crochet embellishment is the perfect way to add interest to any garment. In days gone by, when 'Make do and mend' was the mantra, crochet was often used to make detachable collars and cuffs that transformed plain everyday sweaters into fancy 'Sunday best' or evening wear.*

TENSION

Exact tension is not essential for this pattern.

FINISHED MEASUREMENTS

Collar measures 8 cm wide and approx 70 cm around the inside of the neckline.

A

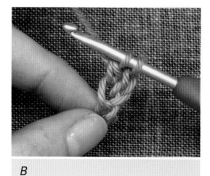

B

C

SPECIAL STITCHES

Vst: *(1tr, 4ch, 1tr) in next st.*

Shell: *([1tr, 2ch] 3 times, 1tr) all in next ch-sp.*

Bobble: ** 3ch, ** yoh, insert hook into bottom of 3ch, **(A)** draw up a loop, yoh and draw through 2 loops **(B)**; rep from ** 4 times, (5 loops on hook), **(C)** yoh and draw through all 5 loops **(D)**. Now repeat from * once more **(E)**. Slip stitch back down into bottom of first 3ch to join bobble **(F)**.*

PATTERN NOTES

❖ *1ch does not count as a dc.*

> ### TIP
> If a plain neckpiece is not for you, experiment with different colours. Play with stripes to create a striking pattern within the collar, or hook the ties and bobbles in a contrasting shade.

D

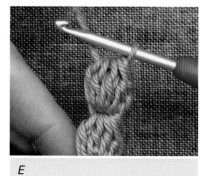

E

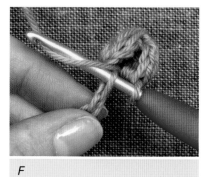

F

PATTERN

With 4 mm hook make 83ch.

Row 1: 1dc in second ch from hook and each ch to end, turn – 82dc.

Row 2: 4ch (counts as 1tr, 1ch), ([1tr, 1ch] twice) all in first dc, miss next dc* (1tr, 1ch) in next dc, miss next dc; rep from * to last dc, ([1tr, 1ch] twice, 1tr) all in last dc, turn – 46tr.

Row 3: 1ch, 1dc in tr, * 2dc in next ch-sp, 1dc in tr; rep from * to end, turn – 136dc.

Row 4: 3ch (counts as tr), 1tr in same st, 2tr in each of next 3 sts, 1tr in each st to last 4 sts, 2tr in each st to end, turn – 144tr.

Row 5: 1ch, 1dc in first tr, * miss 2 tr, 1Vst (see Special Stitches) in next tr, miss 2 tr, 1dc in next tr; rep from * to end, turn – 24Vsts.

Row 6: 1ch, 1 shell (see Special Stitches) in each ch-sp across, 1 dc in last dc, turn – 24 shells.

Row 7: 1ch, 3dc in each ch-sp across.

Do not fasten off, but make a chain of approx 40 cm long, then make a **bobble** (see Special Stitches) at the end of the chain.

Fasten off yarn.

Reattach yarn to opposite end of Collar with a ss and repeat as for first chain and bobble.

FINISHING

Weave in all ends.

Pin and block the collar lightly into shape.

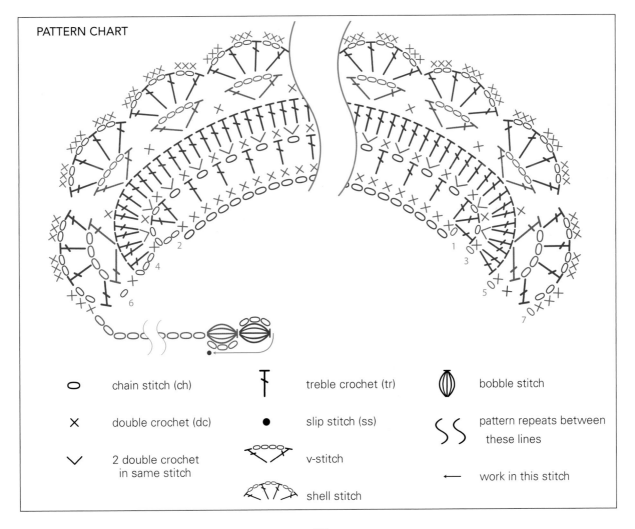

PATTERN CHART

⟳	chain stitch (ch)	𝍎 treble crochet (tr)	⬢ bobble stitch

⟳ chain stitch (ch)

✕ double crochet (dc)

∨ 2 double crochet in same stitch

𝍎 treble crochet (tr)

● slip stitch (ss)

v-stitch

shell stitch

bobble stitch

pattern repeats between these lines

⟵ work in this stitch

Slouchy
BEANIE HAT

Hats are very good beginner projects as they are quick and simple to make. Slouchy beanies are stylish and particularly easy to hook, as they often require less shaping to create the oversized casual look.

MATERIALS

You will need a wool rich DK weight yarn in four colours. Here we have used Louisa Harding™ Grace, 50% Merino wool, 50% silk, 50 g/100 m/ per ball.

    Yarn A: 38 'Dolphin' x 1 ball

    Yarn B: 53 'Fitz' x 1 ball

    Yarn C: 32 'Frost' x 1 ball

    Yarn D: 47 'Tender' x 1 ball

4 mm hook

Yarn needle

YARN ALTERNATIVES

When substituting yarn, the required lengths will vary from one brand of yarn to another. Any DK, wool rich yarn will substitute here, although experimenting with yarn weights and hook sizes will simply cause the hat to come out bigger or smaller. If a hat in a single colour is desired, the total weight of yarn used in the piece is approx 145 g.

STITCH TECHNIQUES

Chain (ch)
Double crochet (dc)
Treble crochet (tr)
Working through back loops only (blo)
Shells
Working in the round (rnd)
Working in rows
Striping
Slip stitch (ss) join
(See also Special Stitches)

GENERAL TIPS

❖ *This hat uses a shell stitch to create texture and allow the colours to fade into each other rather than being separated as strong stripes.*

TENSION

Work 2 pattern repeats and 10 rows to measure 10 x 10 cm using a 4 mm hook or the size needed to obtain the correct tension.

A

B

C

FINISHED MEASUREMENTS

The hat can be adjusted for a bespoke fit. The sample shown is to fit an average woman's head – rib stretching to fit 56 cm circumference.

SPECIAL STITCHES

Shell: *(3tr, 1ch, 3tr) all in next st.*
Dc through back loops only (dcblo): *Insert hook through back loop of each stitch only.*
7trdec (decrease over next 7 sts): *[Yoh, insert in next st, yoh and draw loop through, yoh and draw through 2 loops (A)] 7 times, 8 loops on hook, (B), yoh and draw through all loops on hook (C).*

PATTERN NOTES

❖ *The hat can be adjusted to size. Simply work the rib until it fits snugly around the head – with enough stretch to stay on and not slip down. Then when working from the rib, make sure there are a multiple of 6dc worked.*

PATTERN

Rib
With 4 mm hook and Yarn A, make 11ch.
Row 1: 1dc in second ch from hook and each ch to end, turn – 10dc.
Row 2: 1ch (does not count as stitch), 1dcblo (see Special Stitches) in each dc to end, turn – 10dcblo.
Rep last row until rib is desired length around head. For average woman's head, work 50 cm in length to stretch to fit 54–56 cm head circumference.

Join two short ends of strip together into a ring with a ss join.

Crown
With 4 mm hook and Yarn A, work evenly in dc all round one long edge of rib, ensuring that there are a multiple of 6 sts, join rnd with ss.
For average woman sample shown, there are 102 sts worked.
Rnd 1: 1ch (counts as 1dc), miss 2 dc, shell (see

Special Stitches) in next dc, miss 2 dc, * 1dc in next dc, miss 2 dc, shell in next dc, miss 2 dc; rep from * around, join rnd with ss – 17 shells in average woman sample shown.

Change to yarn B.

Rnd 2: 3ch (counts as 1tr), 2tr in same st, 1dc in next shell, * shell in next dc, 1dc in next shell; rep from * around, (3tr, 1ch) in bottom of first ch, ss to top of ch to join rnd.

Rnd 3: 1ch (counts as 1dc), shell in next dc, * 1dc in next shell, shell in next dc; rep from * around, join rnd with ss.

Rnds 4–6: As Rnds 2 and 3.

Change to yarn C and work 12 rnds in pattern as set.

Change to yarn D and work 2 rnds in pattern as set.

Decrease rnd: 1ch (counts as 1dc), **7trdec** (see Special Stitches), 1ch, * 1dc in next 1ch-sp, 7trdec, 1ch; rep from * around, join rnd with ss.

Fasten off yarn, leaving a tail of at least 20 cm to sew up hole.

Thread yarn through all stitches at top edge, pull up tightly to draw in hole and secure.

Weave in all ends and block the crown very lightly to shape, do not block the ribbing.

TIP

When working the seven treble decrease, be careful not to snag the yarn when drawing through the eight loops at once. Take your time, pull the hook smoothly at a slight angle and if it helps, draw the hook through each loop separately rather than trying to drag it through all the loops quickly at the same time.

PATTERN CHART

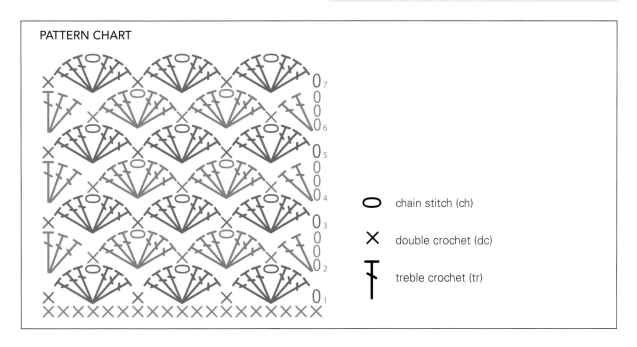

◯   chain stitch (ch)

✕   double crochet (dc)

⊥   treble crochet (tr)

GLOSSARY

Amigurumi The Japanese art of knitting or crocheting small stuffed animals.

Backstitch An easy way to seam your pieces of crochet fabric together. Bring the needle out to the front of the fabric, then bring it back down to the right of that point, creating your first stitch. Bring the needle back out to the front of the fabric to the left of the stitch, the same distance away. Take the needle back down into the fabric through the original point, creating another stitch. Repeat this process along your seam, working from right to left and working each stitch 'back' to the previous one.

Ball band The paper or card attached to your yarn when you buy it. Contains information on the yarn company, fibre content, weight and length of the yarn, and often gives details of suggested hook sizes.

Base chain *See* foundation chain.

Blocking Washing your finished crochet and laying it out to dry. This helps the yarn relax and the stitches settle into their final position. If crocheting lace, you can pin the fabric out when blocking to stretch it and bring out the pattern.

Chain One loop drawn through another loop again and again. Most crochet projects start with a length of foundation chain which the first row of stitches is then worked into.

Chain space (ch-sp) A gap caused by working one or more chain stitches during a row.

Chevron A zig zag pattern created by working set repeats of increases and decreases, which form peaks and troughs across the row.

Cotton A durable natural fibre which is cool and breathable, and takes dyes well.

Dominant hand This is your right hand if you are right-handed, and your left hand if you are left-handed.

Double crochet (dc) The smallest of the regular stitches, which creates a dense fabric.

Double treble (dtr) The next tallest stitch after the treble crochet, worked by adding an extra wrap of yarn at the start of the stitch.

Duplicate stitch A neat way to finish a round when working in spirals, which will eliminate the 'jog' caused by changing colour.

Dye-lot The batch in which a yarn was dyed. Even when dyed in the same colour by the same company, the colours can vary slightly between dye-lots.

Fastening off Securing your yarn at the end of a piece of crochet. Pull up the final loop, then cut the yarn, leaving a long enough length to weave in or seam if needed, and draw the end through. Pull tight.

Fibre What a yarn is made from – this could be anything from wool or cotton to acrylic, silk or mohair. Different fibres are often blended together to create a yarn with the combined properties of several fibres.

Foundation chain The initial chain stitches created when you start a project, which you work your first row of stitches into.

Gauge *See* Tension.

Granny square One of the basic motifs in crochet. There are many variations, but most patterns use clusters of treble stitches with chain stitches to form the corners.

Grip The way you hold your hook as you crochet. The most common are the knife grip and the pencil grip.

Grouped stitches Working multiple crochet stitches into a single stitch or space. Examples of grouped stitches are shells, bobbles, popcorns and puffs.

Half treble crochet (htr) Slightly taller than a double crochet stitch, this creates a drapey fabric that's not too open.

Hook The basic tool for crochet, made of a shaft with a curved hook at the end for pulling the yarn through stitches. Hooks come in many different materials and the size of the shaft affects the size of the stitches.

Jogless stripes When you work crochet in spirals, colour changes will create a 'jog' in the striping, as the yarn changes from one stitch to the next. You can avoid this by using a jogless stripes technique such as duplicate stitch.

Join-as-you-go A method of joining crochet motifs as you work the final round of each motif, rather than seaming them together afterwards.

Mattress stitch This creates the most professional looking seam when finishing your crocheted projects. Use a blunt darning needle, and with the RS of both pieces facing towards you, secure the yarn at the bottom of one piece. Pass the needle to the other section and pick up one stitch. Pull the yarn through and pull tight. Insert the needle through one stitch of the first section, entering where the yarn exited previously. Continue in this way, picking up a stitch first on one side and then the other, as if lacing up a corset, until you reach the last stitch. Secure tightly to finish.

Mohair A fibre made from the hair of angora goats. Mohair is very soft and fluffy but it is hairy and quite 'sticky', meaning it can be tricky to work with and very difficult to rip back if you make mistakes.

Picot Ornamental loops of crochet, often used in edgings.

Plies The individual threads that make up a strand of yarn, spun around each other to create thickness and strength.

Pom-pom maker A plastic tool for quickly and easily making pom-poms. They come in a variety of sizes and can save a lot of time if you are making a number of pom-poms.

Scissors Choose small, sharp scissors for snipping yarn, and heavy fabric scissors if cutting lining fabric or similar.

Shaping Using increases and decreases to change the shape of your work.

Skein Yarn that's been loosely coiled and twisted together. A skein of yarn will need winding into a ball before you begin to crochet or it will get tangled and knotted very quickly.

Slipknot A loop knotted into a length of yarn, which can be made bigger or smaller by pulling on one side of the yarn. The starting point of most crochet projects, creating the first loop on the hook that chains and stitches are then worked from.

Slip stitch (ss) The smallest crochet stitch. This doesn't add any height to the fabric and is often used to join one stitch to another.

Stitch markers Any way of marking a specific stitch in your work. Crochet usually uses either a split ring marker or a lockable marker, which looks like a small padlock, both made of plastic.

Surface crochet Slip stitches worked across the surface of a piece of fabric, often in a different colour to create a decorative effect.

Swatch A sample of fabric, worked to check the tension of your yarn and hook, or to see how a given yarn or stitch pattern will look and drape.

Tapestry needle A blunt sewing needle, used for seaming your crochet and weaving in ends.

Tension The number of stitches and rows a piece of crocheted fabric has. Everyone tends to work to a different tension depending on how they hold the yarn and hook. You can vary your tension by changing the hook size. If you're working garments, or projects where the finished size is important, you need to match the designer's tension. If you're making accessories or soft toys, the tension is less important.

Treble crochet (tr) The tallest of the basic stitches, this creates a fairly open fabric and is used to work the classic granny square pattern.

Turning chain A short length of chain worked at the start of the row, to bring you up to the correct height for working the following stitches. The number of chain stitches depends on the height of the stitches to be worked.

Weight The thickness of the yarn. A laceweight yarn is very fine, while a chunky weight yarn is very thick and will work up quickly on a large hook. The most popular yarn weight is DK, which is a medium weight yarn suitable for a large variety of projects.

Wool Yarn spun from the fleece of sheep. Wool is insulating, strong and breathable. Check if wool is 'superwash', which means it can be machine washed, otherwise it may felt (mat together).

Yarn The thread you crochet with. It can be anything from very fine cotton thread to strips of fabric.

Yarn needle *See* Tapestry needle.

Yoh Yarn over hook.

Zig zag *See* Chevron.

INDEX